MAYNARD
MASSACHUSETTS

MAYNARD
MASSACHUSETTS

· A BRIEF HISTORY ·

THE TOWN OF MAYNARD
SESQUICENTENNIAL STEERING COMMITTEE

Published by The History Press
Charleston, SC
www.historypress.com

Photographs were taken by David A. Mark unless otherwise noted.

First published 2020

ISBN 9781540245434

Library of Congress Control Number: 2020941949

Notice: The information in this book is true and complete to the best of our knowledge. It is offered without guarantee on the part of the author or The History Press. The author and The History Press disclaim all liability in connection with the use of this book.

CONTENTS

Contents

Contents

ACKNOWLEDGEMENTS

The Sesquicentennial Steering Committee wishes to acknowledge the assistance that has come from numerous sources. Among these are the following: Maynard Historical Society, Maynard Historical Commission, Maynard Public Library (for its collection of Town of Maynard annual reports and microfilm of newspapers), Stow Historical Society and Sudbury Historical Society. The historical societies, through tedious labor by volunteers, have collected, catalogued, scanned and computerized a vast collection of artifacts, documents and photographs.

Thanks to the descendants of Amory and Mary Maynard for providing documents and photos pertaining to the family. Thanks to the members of the Maynard Historical Committee who compiled the centennial book in 1971: Beverly G. Allan, Winnifred G. Hearon, Birger R. Koski, Elizabeth M. Schnair and Ralph L Sheridan. Thanks to the authors of previously published books about the history of Maynard and its predecessor towns of Sudbury and Stow: Paul Boothroyd, William Gutteridge, Lewis Halprin, Alfred Hudson, Lisa A. Liedes, David A. Mark, Edwin Way Teale, Jan Voogd and Ann Zwinger. Thanks to the people who have published books and other materials about Digital Equipment Corporation: Reesa E. Abrams, David Allison, Elisabeth Coen, Alan R. Earls, David Thomas Goodwin, W.C. Hanson, Jamie Parker Pearson, Edgar Schein, Barbara A. Walker and the Computer History Museum. Kelly Dennis, a Nipmuc-descendant Native American, provided content and advice for the section "Before the Europeans Arrived…and After."

Acknowledgements

Images derive from the collection of the Maynard Historical Society, as well as contemporary work by Maynard photographer David Mark and other sources.

Without the valuable assistance of all of these public-spirited organizations and people, this project could not have been accomplished.

INTRODUCTION

As we approach the 150th anniversary of the creation of Maynard, it's worth asking: How much history can be written about one small town? This book does not replace the fifty-year history book by W.H. Gutteridge or the centennial history *History of Maynard, Massachusetts, 1871–1971*. Rather, it sets the table with chapters summarizing the history of the first one hundred years and then plunges into in-depth content about what has happened in the following fifty years, plus a crystal ball peek at what might happen in the next fifty. Together, the text and images provide a frame of reference for the people of Maynard to understand where we are now and how we got there.

Chapter 1
BECOMING MAYNARD

Maynard is different from neighboring towns in several ways—it is smaller in area, and its founding as a named town came one to two centuries later compared to Concord, Sudbury, Stow and Acton. From the beginning, it was part of the Industrial Revolution, whereas its neighbors were colonial-era farm towns. The very creation of Maynard came about because its population growth took place at the border between Sudbury and Stow and, thus, quite far from the churches and schools at the centers of those towns.

TERRAIN

Maynard's geology is the result of being repeatedly run over by ice age glaciers one to two miles thick. There are still outcroppings of bedrock, but most of what a person with a shovel will encounter under a layer of topsoil are glacial deposits ranging from silt up to sizable boulders. All this was either deposited by advancing ice or else moved by millennia of glacial melt followed by millennia of post-glacial water erosion from rain and snowmelt. The last glacial expansion period started about 115,000 years ago, reached a glacial maximum 23,000 years ago and then took about 12,000 years to melt, leaving us with mile-thick ice only at Greenland.

Forward-moving glaciers erode terrain through two principal processes: plucking and abrasion. The first involves meltwater seeping into cracks in the bedrock and then freezing. Expansion through freezing breaks rocks loose, which are then rounded by being dragged across the bedrock. Rocks of all sizes—fist-sized up to car- and even bus-sized—can be moved hundreds of miles. Large rocks on the surface are referred to as glacial erratics. Examples of these can be found along Maynard's woodland trails. Smaller edge-rounded rocks numbering in the billions make up New England's stone walls and house foundations. Abrasion occurs when the rock burden of the underside of the glacier acts like sandpaper, smoothing the bedrock while creating stone dust that becomes deposits of clay after water melt transportation. Rock fragments and soil are also deposited on the tops of glaciers, the result of mountain rock slides and soil erosion. These settle in place as the ice melts. Windborne dust and sand (i.e., "aeolian deposits," referred to as "loess") also contribute more to soil building.

Drumlins (oval-shaped hills) are created underneath advancing ice. Summer Hill and other large hills in Maynard are drumlins. In contrast, kames (pronounced as one syllable) are composed of sand, gravel and rocks deposited by glacial melt. These can be mounds, terraces flanking river valleys, deltas and eskers. Porous glacial debris filled valleys, becoming the aquifers that are tapped for Maynard's well water supply. Undraining areas over shallow bedrock became swamps and wetlands. Flattish areas with better drainage supported plant growth that, in turn, decayed to soil suitable for farming. Hills developed a thin mantle of topsoil supporting forests that were, once cleared, suitable for pasture but prone to erosion. Hill farmers complained that each spring saw a "crop" of rocks rising to the surface, but what was really happening was that subsurface rocks were exposed by continual erosion, accelerated when land was cleared and plowed for planting.

Imagine, then, a post-glacial tundra landscape covered in lichen, shrubs and moss around the shores of glacial lakes, transitioning in time to annual plants and scrubs, then spruce/hemlock/pine forest and then mixed forest. Animal life expanded north as temperatures moderated. Humans, who had crossed from northern Asia to the North American continent about fifteen thousand years ago, reached the New England region roughly five thousand years later. From this period, deemed Early Archaic, archaeological finds include spear points and hide scrapers, testimony for the presence of a sparsely populated hunter-gatherer civilization. Going forward, the gradual addition of agriculture—initially corn and then squash, beans and tobacco—meant that the floodplains and more level land became preferred for farming. Periodic deliberate burning of underbrush created open forests

In geological terms, an erratic is material moved by geologic forces from one location to another, sometimes hundreds of miles, usually by a glacier. This boulder is in the Assabet River Walk woods.

with easy passage along trails and better sightlines for hunting game, with said game (deer, elk, bison) grazing on the grasses and saplings that flourished in the increased sunlight. When the European colonists arrived, they were amazed at the openness of the woodlands that allowed easy travel by horse.

BEFORE THE EUROPEANS ARRIVED...AND AFTER

Prior to the arrival of the Europeans, the native population of what is now central Massachusetts, from around Concord west to Springfield, were the Nipmucs, who may have numbered as many as eight thousand. *Nipmuc* has many alternative spellings, such as *Nipmug*, *Neetmock* and *Nipnet*, all generally accepted as translating to "fresh water people." The Nipmucs were part of the much geographically larger area of peoples who spoke various Algonquian dialects, had trade alliances with neighboring tribes and also with the English colonists, the latter primarily for fur trading. Their neighbors were the Pequots to the south, Wampanoags to the southeast, Massachusetts to the east, Pennacooks to the north and Pocumtucs to the west. The Nipmucs grew corn and other crops, hunted deer and moose and, in the spring, enjoyed the bounty of herring, alewives and shad swimming upriver to spawn. Berries and nuts were gathered in their seasons.

To archaeologists, this was the Woodlands period (from three thousand years ago to the arrival of Europeans), with artifacts including pottery and arrowheads and the culture a combination of agriculture, hunting and gathering. Thousands of years earlier, after the melt-back of the last ice age, Paleolithic hunters wandered this area when it was a treeless tundra. Century upon century, plant growth increased and decayed, creating topsoil that would support forests. This older period is referred to as Early Archaic, superseded by Late Archaic. An archaeological dig called "Pine Hawk" documented stone artifacts discovered from the Archaic periods—primarily spear points and hide scrapers—as well as fire pits and small mounds of freshwater mussel shells, when Acton was surveying land for a wastewater treatment facility.

The subsequent Woodland culture involved movement within a village's territory, basically relocating to be near seasonal food sources. There was agriculture and trade. Intermittent warfare could result in tribute paid to

These Native American flint points were found on Maynard farmland in the 1930s. *Courtesy of Maynard Historical Society.*

neighboring tribes. To the west of the Nipmuc region, there was chronic low-level warfare with the Mohawks. One recourse was to build wooden stockades of tree trunks stuck vertically in the ground, with sleeping huts within the stockade. This protected against night attacks and provided a haven during day attacks. There is scant evidence in Maynard, however, of inhabitants during the Woodland period. The land, then and now, was hilly and not well suited for agriculture. The Assabet River was fast-moving in the spring and then very shallow in the summer and fall, so it was less conducive to year-round fishing compared to the Sudbury and Concord Rivers.

Wherever Europeans arrived in what became New England, within a generation entire cultures and populations were wiped out. The initial causes have historically been attributed to a litany of diseases, including smallpox, plague, yellow fever, measles, influenza, scarlet fever and more. However, more recently, *Leptospira*, a bacterium, has been tentatively identified as the cause of the first, and worst, epidemic of 1616–19. This bacteria species infects humans and other mammals. Infection is through ingesting contaminated water or via skin exposure to it if there are open wounds, even minor ones such as nicks and scratches. Native Americans were at risk because they were in and out of water to catch fish, play and bathe. Severe leptospirosis can cause liver, kidney, lungs and brain damage. Signs and symptoms include fever, muscle weakness, dehydration, intense headache, jaundice due to liver failure and hemorrhagic bleeding in the respiratory and digestive systems. Infection and death swept through villages so quickly that the living did not have time to bury the dead. The natives referred to the event as the "Great Dying." The Pilgrims and subsequent English settlers described finding empty villages with bones scattered on the ground.

As a result, the Puritans who made up the "Great Migration" from England, between 1620 and 1640, found this to be "empty" land that had until recent years been partially cleared and farmed by the native populations. This was easily returned to productive farmland—a process of combining the native crops of corn, beans and squash with European wheat and an assortment of edible domesticated animals (cattle, hogs, sheep, goats and chickens). With crops suitable for winter storage plus domesticated animals to eat, the colonists did not have to rely so heavily on hunting or practice the seminomadic lifestyle of the natives. Instead, they owned and farmed in place.

There were subsequent native epidemics from other diseases in 1631–33, 1645, 1650–52 and 1670—compounded by exclusion from traditional lands and outright war. The depopulation by disease was thought of by the English as divine intervention. King James I is quoted as saying, "There hath, by God's visitation, reigned a wonderful plague, the utter destruction, devastation, and depopulation of that whole territory." Before contact with Europeans, the Algonquin region that extended from Long Island to Maine numbered 100,000 to 150,000 people. One hundred years later, it was one-twentieth of that.

The Puritans were firm believers in Christianity and farming—in that order. Some of the native peoples who had survived the diseases converted and gathered into what were referred to as the "Praying Indian Villages." One of these was Nashobah, now Littleton. What is now Maynard and eastern Stow went by the name Pompositticut, said to mean "land of many hills." It was not part of any subsequently Christianized village.

Transfer and Taking of Land

Transfer of land from natives to English settlers was a combination of sale, forced sale, encroachment and outright taking. From the colonial side, the governor and General Court of the Colony of Massachusetts would grant a group a right to settle an area of land. The grantees were obliged to occupy the land and pursue obtaining a deed of sale from Native Americans. In 1635, Concord was approved, with an area of thirty-six square miles. The purchase was competed in 1637. Squa Sachem, Tahattawan, Nimrod and others accepted payment from Simon Willard, John Jones and others. Payment was *wampum*, steel tools and clothing. (*Wampum* was a shortening of *wampumpeag*, a native word meaning "white strings of shell beads." The beads, tediously handmade from whelk shells, were legal tender between the Commonwealth of Massachusetts and Native Americans.) Many years later, two Native Americans—Peter Jethro and Jehojakin—having witnessed the sale, provided testimony that it had been a fair bargain.

In 1638, Sudbury was granted a right to create a town of twenty-five square miles. The deed of purchase was registered in 1648. A subsequent expansion to the west in 1649 was referred to as the "Two-Mile Grant." This reached to the Assabet River, thus including land that in 1871 became the south side of Maynard. While granted and divided into 130-acre lots, much of this was not occupied at that time. Attempts at clearing and farming were halted by King Philip's War, which also included the destruction of much of Sudbury proper.

A forced transfer of land of what became Maynard was between Tantamous, also called "Old Jethro" (father of Peter Jethro), who lived at Nobscot, now the Framingham/Sudbury border. In 1651, Tantamous was forced to surrender claim to one thousand acres west of the Sudbury grant to Hermon Garrett, of Concord, in a court dispute over payment for the purchase of two horses. Separately, Pompositticut Plantation, west of Concord—later to become Stow—was surveyed circa 1660 (described as "meane land") and granted, but as not permanently settled at that time, as the grant later rescinded.

All this granting and purchasing crashed to an end with King Philip's War of 1675–76. Metacom, also known as Metacomet and by the English name Philip, was a Wampanoag chief. (Native chiefs often assumed English names.) Attempts to maintain a truce between the Wampanoags and the English colonists were frayed by colonial expansion and scattered acts of violence on both sides. In the summer of 1675, the actions of the Native Americans coalesced into concerted attacks on towns across the Plymouth, Massachusetts Bay, Rhode Island, New Haven and Connecticut colonies. Locally, history has it that Metacom's supporters met atop Pompositticut Hill—now Summer Hill—to decide whether to attack Concord or Sudbury (the answer: Sudbury).

Although the colonial militias were supplemented by volunteers from the Praying Villages, there was suspicion that Nipmucs were also collaborating with King Philip. This was in part true. The Nipmucs understood the threat of colonial expansion. Additionally, Metacom's Wampanoag warriors were residing in Nipmuc territory much of the summer and fall of 1675. To remove this perceived threat, natives were restricted by the colonists to five of the Praying Villages, and then, in October 1675, hundreds were relocated to Deer Island, in Boston Harbor. Winter weather combined with inadequate housing and shortage of food led to more than half dying there. Tantamous and his family either escaped from Deer Island or had avoided being sent there. Although he was more along the way of being a noncombatant refugee, Tantamous was captured in New Hampshire, marched through Boston with a noose on his neck and hanged in the Boston Common. His family, other than Peter Jethro, were sold into slavery.

In 1676, Metacom was shot and his body drawn and quartered; his head was put on display in Plymouth for many years. Prisoners of war, including his wife and young son, were transported to Caribbean islands and sold as slaves there. Returning ships sometimes brought African-born slaves from the islands to sell in New England, slavery having been legalized by the

The Council of Algonquin Indians of New England met annually for several years in the 1920s, seen here in a 1924 photograph. In the middle of the second row is James Lemuel Cisco (1846–1931), who had taken on role of chief of the Hassanamisco Band of Nipmuc. Seated at the left end is his daughter, Sarah Cisco Sullivan. She and her daughter, Zara Cisco Brough, continued stewardship of the reservation and tribal leadership. *Photo by L.W. Thurston, Providence, Rhode Island.*

Colony of Massachusetts in 1640. Many of the Nipmucs who survived this catastrophe moved north or west and were assimilated into other tribes.

Those who remained behind were confined to Praying Villages and reservations. The Commonwealth of Massachusetts recognizes the present-day Nipmucs as constituting a group of some five hundred members living in and around the city of Worcester, Chaubunagungamaug Reservation (in Thompson, Connecticut) and Hassanamisco Reservation (in Grafton, Massachusetts). The reservations are small plots of land without permanent residents, used by tribal members of the present-day Nipmuc and other Native American people for gatherings and celebrations.

Colonial settlement was renewed in 1678, leading to a May 1683 General Court approval of a town name "Stow," an eastern chunk of which was sold in 1871 to create Maynard. In 1684, deeds to this and the Two-Mile

Grant for northwest Sudbury, also to become part of Maynard, were signed by a dozen or so Native Americans who were among a postwar remnant population, including Peter Jethro. Land taking continued elsewhere. The Hassanamesit Reservation had contained 7,500 acres in 1728 when the Commonwealth of Massachusetts purchased most of the land. The money from the sale was to be held for the Nipmucs in an account at a Boston bank, but it was embezzled by a state official. Only in 1869 did the Massachusetts legislature pass a law granting citizenship to the descendants through the Massachusetts Indian Enfranchisement Act.

EARLY SETTLERS, EARLY ROADS

William Brown's farm was the first documented residence on land that would in time become Maynard. He had settled in 1650 on what was the northwest part of Sudbury's "Two-Mile Grant." History does not tell whether he had to abandon the homestead during King Philip's War of 1675–76, but that is likely. His family returned—the George Brown house at 93 Acton Street, built in 1830, is on part of the original farm. North of this is the Marble Farm historic site, marked by a plaque next to the Assabet River Rail Trail. The Marble family moved here from Andover, Massachusetts, around 1705 (this is disputed, as there are claims for as early as 1683). The family lived there until the house burned in 1924. Various maps show it as the Marble, Whitney or Parmenter farm because a Marble daughter married a Whitney and then a Whitney daughter married a Parmenter. All three of these family names date their arrival in the colonies to the 1630s.

The Smiths were also early settlers here and in time owned much of what would become Maynard, especially along Great Road. Some of what still stand as the oldest houses in town once belonged to Thomas, Haman, Amos, Benjamin, Jonathan, William, George or Dexter Smith, all descendants of a John Smith who had come from England in 1638. Glenwood Cemetery holds graves of at least sixty Smiths, and there are dozens of people with last name Smith living in Maynard today. When Amory Maynard moved here, much of the land he was buying was from the Smiths. The dam across the Assabet River is called the Ben Smith Dam because it was on land Amory bought from Ben Smith.

There are close to a dozen Maynard-named people buried at Glenwood Cemetery who were not descendants or married to descendants of Amory

Steps to the basement of what had been the Marble family homestead were hand tool–shaped from granite boulders. Before a 2009 Boy Scout cleanup, the bottom half of the flight had been under dirt naturally composted from nearly a century of leaf fall.

and Mary Maynard. Amory's great-great-great-great-grandfather crossed the Atlantic Ocean in 1638. He and his descendants had many children. The non-Amory Maynards in Maynard were distant relatives who had settled from Sudbury. Other early settler names include Puffer (of Puffer Pond, in the wildlife refuge), Balcom, Rice, Wood, Brigham, Brooks, Gibson, Vose, Whitney and Conant.

Many of the old roads are still with us. Lancaster Road connected Sudbury to Lancaster, passing through the center of Stow. A part of this route is now named White Pond Road. The present-day bridge over the Assabet River, located on the Maynard/Stow border, is at a bridge site dating back to 1715 (replaced in 1800, 1929 and 2007). When it was first built, there was no other bridge over the Assabet between it and Concord.

South of the river, Old Marlborough Road connected Concord to Marlborough. Although already old and abandoned by Henry David Thoreau's time, parts still exist in Maynard as "Old Marlboro Road." Rice Tavern stood at the crossroads of the Lancaster and Marlborough Roads.

The standing stone commemorating the minutemen march was dedicated in June 1976. *From left to right*: Massachusetts legislator William C. Mullin, Town of Maynard selectmen Richard T. White and Captain Walter Mattson of the Assabet Valley Minutemen. *Courtesy of Maynard Historical Society.*

Remains of the foundation can be seen just inside the Assabet River National Wildlife Refuge, from the Old Marlboro Road entrance.

North of the river, Concord Road connected Stow to Concord. This road was the path for Stow's minutemen marching to Concord to confront the British troops the morning of April 19, 1775. A modest stone marker on Concord Road, next to the Haynes water trough, commemorates the event. The march is reenacted every April, with a 5:00 a.m. pause at the Concord and Acton Streets intersection to fire a rifle volley.

Somewhat newer was the Boston Post Road, also known as Great Road (and now known as Route 117). This crossed what would become Maynard from east to west, spanning the Assabet River on a bridge constructed in 1816, replaced in 1922 and overdue for replacement again. This was a stagecoach and mail route from Boston to points west.

With all these roads passing through, was there a population center that became a nascent Assabet village? Not really. Southeast of the Assabet River was the northern fringe of Sudbury, with about a dozen homesteads. Northwest of the river was the east edge of Stow, likewise sparsely settled. Only after Amory Maynard and William Knight appeared on the scene with folding money in their pockets and a vision of a woolen mill did the population start to grow. Main Street, with a bridge over the river, dates to 1849. It was the first Maynard street to be paved with asphalt, in 1897.

HOW ASSABET VILLAGE BECAME A MILL TOWN

Crossing Maynard from west to east, the Assabet River travels 2.4 miles and drops thirty-five feet. The volume and vertical drop were enough to initially power two mills that doubled as sawmills and gristmills (for grain), later converted to factory mills. Upriver, there were three more river-spanning mills, the closest at Gleasondale, and one more downriver in West Concord. The same steep, hilly landscape that made the area poor for farming made it right for mills, and hence for people to work in mills, and hence a mill town.

Sawmills and Gristmills

During the colonial expansion in from the coast, the first mills to appear were typically sawmills, followed by gristmills. Sometimes one mill served both purposes, powering a saw in the spring, when the tree trunks cut and transported in winter would be sawn into beams, planks and so on. Come fall, the water wheel would power millstones that would grind the farmers' corn and wheat. One such multipurpose mill was sited at what became Mill Street, with the earliest owners identified as Gibson and then Jewel (or Jewell?). A bridge constructed in 1816 was Jewel's Mill Bridge. The mill was converted to powering the manufacture of wooden spindles for textile mills and came to be owned by Asa Smith.

On the eastern edge of what would become Maynard, another sawmill was constructed circa 1800 that in 1835 would be converted in a gunpowder production facility. The dam is in Acton, but the backed-up water—Ripple Pond—and part of the sprawl of facilities crossed west into what was then called Powder Mill Village, now the eastern-most part of Maynard. Gunpowder manufacturing remained in operation into World War II. Over the course of the century, there were twenty-six documented explosions, tallying thirty fatalities.

There were also a few saw- and gristmills that had no potential for being industrially repurposed. These were on Taylor Brook, a tributary to the Assabet that drained from Puffer Pond, now all in the Assabet River National Wildlife Refuge. Taylor Brook reaches the Assabet just west of Ice House Landing, into a small body of water called "Thanksgiving Pond," so named because it was often frozen over and suitable for ice skating by Thanksgiving.

In late 1845, partners William H. Knight and Amory Maynard descended on the town with the intention of buying up land and water rights and creating a wool mill business. Knight bought the spindles mill, its dam, its water rights and the associated house (still standing as 84 Summer Hill Road) from Asa Smith. Maynard moved his family into the house from Marlborough, his first of three residences in what would become Maynard, and bought lots of land from the Smith and Brooks families. By

A press mill at the gunpowder facility. The photo was taken during the dismantling of the building (hence no walls). Moistened charcoal, sulfur and saltpeter were mixed for hours beneath the two rotating wheels. In operation, workers would periodically add water to reduce the risk of explosion. *Courtesy of Maynard Historical Society.*

November 1846, the partners owned 109 acres of what would become the mill, millpond, canal and Ben Smith Dam.

Here was the process. What is now the millpond was a swamp that drained eastward into the Assabet River. Soil was dredged from the swamp to create a wide swath of dry ground bordering the river. Stone walls kept this from eroding into the river or back into the swamp. Meanwhile, the Ben Smith Dam was built to create a reservoir backing water to and beyond the White Pond Bridge. A canal was dug to connect the reservoir to the newly created millpond. By building the dam upriver from what had been dam for Jewel's mill and building the woolen mill downstream, this created a higher vertical drop for the water, providing much more power from the same volume. Amory Maynard built the first mill building, a wooden structure fifty by one hundred feet in size. Powered by a water wheel, it was producing wool yarn and wool carpets by the spring of 1847.

There is both a simple answer to the beginning of Knight and Maynard appearing in the affairs of Assabet Village and a more complicated answer.

Knight sold his Framingham Long Pond water rights to Boston in 1846 and Maynard his rights to his Marlborough millpond (later named Fort Meadow Reservoir) in 1847, but according to Town of Sudbury records, the interests of the two men turned to the Assabet as early as 1843. Minutes of a town meeting have Knight petitioning the town to create a road that is now Main Street, the purpose being to bring raw wool in and finished goods out from an intended factory. The petition failed. Knight tried again in 1844. That failed as well. In 1845 he petitioned to move the Stow/Sudbury border south so that the center of Assabet Village (and the intended factory site) would be entirely in Stow. Stow supported the petition. It failed nonetheless. But in 1849, a few years after Knight and Maynard built the wool works, Sudbury constructed that road, including a bridge over the Assabet River.

Paper Mill

William May built a paper mill on the Sudbury side of the Assabet River in 1820. This means that in the land that would become Maynard, the first "factory" dam on the Assabet River was not for Maynard's wool mill (1846) or Pratt's gunpowder mill (1835) but rather the paper mill's dam, years earlier. The location was just upstream of the Waltham Street bridge, south side. May sold to John Sawyer, who in turn sold the mill to William Parker. In February 1831, Parker and his partners incorporated the operation as the Fourdrinier Paper Company, selling newsprint paper to the *Boston Journal* and other newspapers. Parker's mill was originally powered by a water wheel and later by coal-fired steam engine. The historic etching of an aerial view of the town of Maynard, dated 1879, shows a sizable mill and a smoke-emitting chimney.

In 1840, a bridge was constructed just downstream from the mill, then called the Paper Mill Bridge. Looking upriver from the bridge gave a fine view of the Paper Mill Dam. The dam and bridge were both destroyed in the flood of 1927. The mill closed in 1882, was used as a warehouse for the Assabet Woolen Company and then burned to the ground on May 14, 1894 (arson was suspected). All that remained was the chimney, which stood "as a gloomy monument to the past" for twenty years more. After the flood, the bridge was rebuilt in 1928; that bridge was replaced in 2013.

The gunpowder mill, paper mill and especially woolen mill all outgrew the power demands that could be met by hydropower alone, and so coal-fired steam engines were installed. By then, the critical components that fostered

The paper mill dam, a short distance upstream from the Waltham Street bridge, was known as "The Falls" for the way water cascaded down the rough stone face. Remnant stones are visible in the river. *Courtesy of Maynard Historical Society.*

more growth were the railroad (to bring raw materials and fuel in and finished goods out) and high-density housing (boardinghouses, apartments, small homes on small lots) that allowed a workforce to walk to and from work. The hamlet "Assabet Village" grew to a population of 1,800 people by the time it became Maynard in 1871. Years after factories left New England for points south and then overseas, former mill towns still have a look and feel distinguishing them from former farm towns.

How Maynard Became Maynard

Maynard was carved out of Sudbury and Stow in April 1871, which explains why it is so much "newer" than those towns, founded in 1639 and 1683, respectively. Before 1871, everything north of the Assabet River was part of Stow and everything south of the river part of Sudbury. Maynard's boundary consists of five straight lines forming a five-sided polygon, 8.27 miles total length, surrounding a land area of 5.4 square miles. The Massachusetts State Acts of 1871, Chapter 198, describes in detail how the lines were drawn. The farmland of the "late" Daniel Whitney (he had died in 1870) extended northwest from what is now Route 27, along what was then the Acton/Stow border. This northernmost stone marker is deep in the woods north of the end of Rockland Avenue.

Heading southwest, the next corner is on the hilltop in the apple orchard bordering the north side of Maynard's Summer Street. The south-heading line went to the Puffer family farm. This marker is in the Assabet River National Wildlife Refuge. The eastward line crosses Puffer Pond to end at a stone marker adjacent to Route 27. The northeastward line ends at a point just off Sudbury Road, about one third of a mile south of where Sudbury Road meets Powder Mill Road.

The northeast border was the preexisting border between the town of Acton and the towns of Sudbury and Stow, established in 1735 when Acton separated from Concord. In fact, there is a line marker just north of the Assabet River, with an "A" on one side and an "S" (for Stow) on the other, because its placement predates the founding of Maynard. The other lines

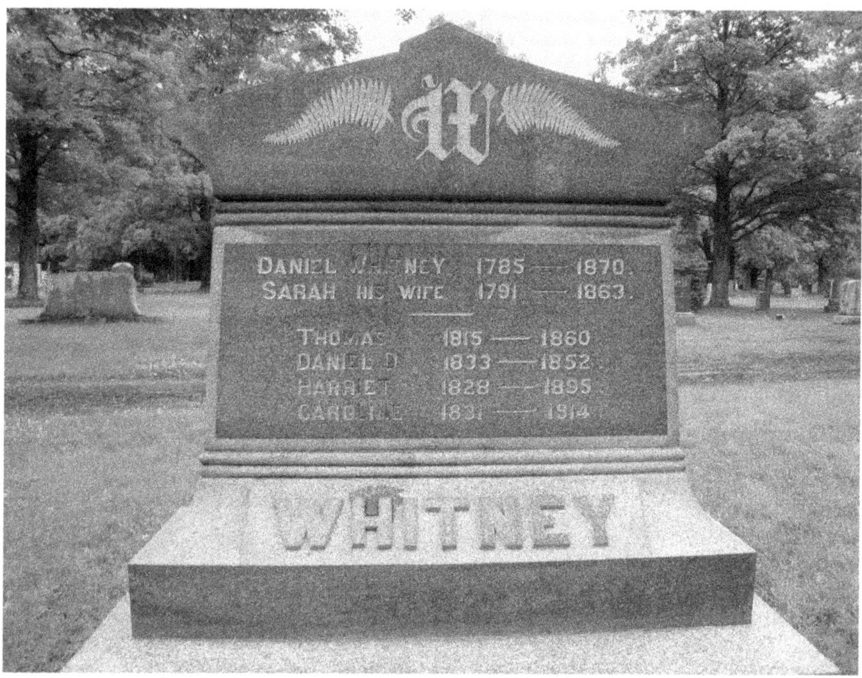

Sarah Whitney's maiden name was Marble. Joseph Marble, her great-great-grandfather, had moved from Andover to what was then part of Sudbury around 1705. Sarah's daughter, Mary, married Joel Parmenter. In Maynard records, the site is referred to as the Marble/Whitney/Parmenter homestead. The foundation of the house (which burned in 1924) is adjacent to the Assabet River Rail Trail.

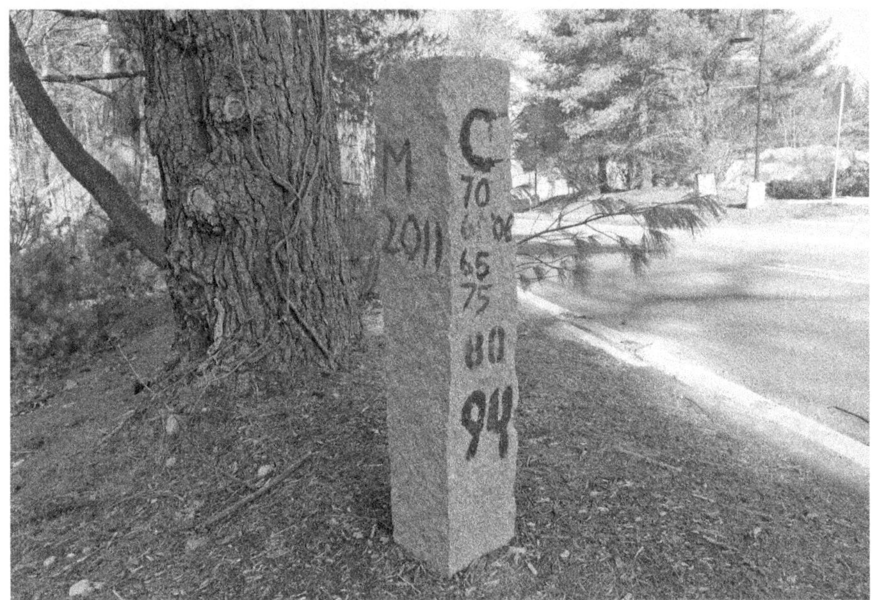

Town officials from Maynard and its neighbors are not actually walking the boundaries, but from this cornerstone, it appears that Concord was more diligent—at least for a while—in documenting its visits to the marker. The other two sides of the stone show "A" for Action and "S" for Sudbury. The stone marks the easternmost corner of Maynard.

were new creations. Maynard started with a population of about eight hundred people from Stow and nine hundred people from Sudbury.

A 1904 atlas of the boundaries of the towns of Middlesex Country provided longitude and latitude for each of the five corners, a description of location relative to then-current landmarks—some long since gone—and physical descriptions of stone markers erected at each corner. Recent visits confirmed that four of the five markers are exactly as described in the atlas. The southernmost stone was replaced by the U.S. Army in 1942 with a granite block embedded flush to the ground. The top of the original stone, incised with the appropriate letters, is in the possession of the Maynard Historical Society.

Maynard's town officials, or their representatives, are supposed to "perambulate the bounds" and paint the year onto the existing stone markers every five years. From a photo of one of the markers, clearly Maynard has missed a few visits. Acton, Concord, Stow and Sudbury have been more diligent.

THE PETITIONS FOR AND AGAINST CREATION OF MAYNARD

How Maynard's boundaries were set is an interesting question. There were some exploratory town-founding rumblings in 1869–70. In an undated petition with sixty-eight signatures—never submitted to the state—the name of the proposed town was left blank. That petition proposed to take land from four towns—Acton, Concord, Sudbury and Stow—and listed the gunpowder mill along with the paper mill and wool mill.

The official petition to the Commonwealth of Massachusetts, proposing to take land only from Sudbury and Stow, was signed by seventy-one men and dated January 26, 1871. While some town histories refer only to the members of this list as the founders of Maynard, three subsequent supportive petitions with sixty-three additional signers were submitted in January and February. Adding the names appended to the unsubmitted petition, collectively nearly two hundred signatures were gathered (there were a few duplications). Among the signatories were men associated with each of the three mills: Nathan Pratt, William Parker and Lorenzo Maynard. Interestingly, Amory Maynard's signature does not appear on any of the petitions.

Key points of the complaint were that the fast-growing population clustered around the mills on the Assabet River was miles away from the town centers of Sudbury and Stow and was not getting adequate school and street improvement spending despite taxes being paid to the parent towns.

The official petition's proposed borders were not the same as what was approved a few months later. What was proposed was much larger—a Greater Maynard. The following description from the January petition starts at what is currently the northern corner of Maynard and works its way counterclockwise back to the starting point:

> *Beginning at the North West corner of the farm of the late Daniel Whitney, thence running Southerly to the road Westerly of the house of Jonathan P. Bent; thence more easterly on a straight line to the town line separating Stow from Hudson; thence Easterly on said line town line to the South East corner of Stow; thence North Easterly on a straight line crossing Bottomless and Willis' Pond to the Concord town line, at or near the place familiarly known as Dungee Hole; thence North Westerly on said town line of Concord & on the town line of Acton to the point of beginning.*

Maynard Historical Society members David Griffin (*left*) and Paul Boothroyd (*right*) accept the donation of the initial, not-submitted petition to form a new town out of parts of Sudbury, Stow, Acton and Concord.

The vague part of the description is determining where the proposed border line would reach the Concord town line, as there is no current map showing Bottomless Pond, nor a place "familiarly known as Dungee Hole." However, we know the former became Crystal Pond, and Henry David Thoreau's journal mentions "Dunge Hole" as a hollow near Concord's White Pond. A Concord map dated 1906 has Dunge Hole Brook as close to where Route 117 crosses the Concord/Sudbury border. Looking at a map, a straight line can indeed be drawn from the southeast corner of Stow to the Concord border at Route 117, bisecting both ponds on the way.

The net result of these proposed borders would have been A) a bit more land left to Stow on the northeast border, B) Maynard getting a larger piece of southeast Stow and C) a much larger part of north Sudbury going to Maynard. This Greater Maynard, even without taking any land from Acton or Concord, would still have been nearly twice the town's present-day size.

To Be or Not to Be?

There was opposition to the petition for the creation of Maynard. Stow residents countered with three remonstrances (petitions against), stating, among other things, that such a division would remove "the only portion that has increased in its population and in its valuation for the past ten years" and also noting that such a sundering "would leave our ancient town in a weak and crippled condition to which we most decidedly object." The remonstrances were signed by a total of 160 of Stow's residents.

On January 23, 1871, Sudbury residents voted 183 to 88 against allowing part of the town to split off and formed a committee "to use all honorable means which in their judgment will aid in preventing the formation of a new town." After the fact, the same committee was assigned to get the best financial settlement.

Maynard prevailed, but with compromises. The way Paul Boothroyd, well-known Maynard history buff, put it, "the Brigham brothers and Webster Cutting wanted to be part of the new town, but Sudbury hired the surveyors who drew the final, smaller border." As indirect support of this theory, Sudbury's town meeting record from April 1872 states, "We have attended to making a survey and establishing a line between said towns…we have also erected stone monuments marked S. & M. at such places as said line crosses the highways."

A visit was made to the Commonwealth of Massachusetts Archives in an attempt to find official documents pertaining to the boundary lines dispute. A collection of original documents referred to as Legislative Packet 1871, Chapter 198, contained the four petitions in support of the proposed formation of Maynard, the three remonstrances from Stow residents opposing the action and the bill dated April 19, 1871, approving the action with the finalized (i.e., present-day) boundary lines. There was no documentation in the Chapter 198 packet to shed light on the changes from the petition to the final boundary lines.

Thus, Maynard was founded on April 19, 1871, twenty-four years after the founding of the carpet mill. According to the book *History of Maynard, 1871–1891*, the new name was chosen to honor mill founder Amory Maynard by unanimous vote of the citizens. However, it is not entirely clear when this "vote" was taken, as the official petition had already stipulated that the new town bear the name Maynard.

THE PRICE OF BECOMING A TOWN

The towns losing land agreed to accept payments. Stow received $6,500 plus interest (totaling $1,470) spread out over seven years. Sudbury received $20,883.28 initially plus $2,700 as $300 per year over nine years, for support of the poor. Sudbury got more than Stow because the wool and paper mills and railroad were in Sudbury and because the initial payment included $10,400 for 104 shares of town-owned stock in the Fitchburg Railroad. Payment documentation is found in Maynard's early annual reports, with the 1880–81 annual report confirming the final payment to Sudbury. To put these payments in context, a woman teacher's salary was $360 per year, and a man's pay for road building was $1.75 per day.

Maynard threw a big party to celebrate its formation. How is this known? Because the treasurer's report in the first annual report itemizes, among other costs, $34.13 for fireworks, $30.00 for a band, $32.65 for "use of cannons" and $14.00 for three kegs of gunpowder.

Interestingly, Sudbury's town meeting records from April 1872 show that the Town of Maynard went through a bit of buyer's remorse. Maynard, it appears, petitioned the state legislature to "relieve them from a fulfillment of their obligations to the town of Sudbury." As Maynard had already paid the $20,883.28 on October 6, 1871, this could only mean that Maynard wanted out of the remaining $2,700 to be paid out over nine years. Maynard lost.

Horses were still a common sight on the streets of Maynard circa 1920. *Courtesy of Maynard Historical Society.*

Sudbury's representatives opposed the petition before the state legislature, which ruled in their favor.

According to the 1871 census for Maynard, the newly minted town started with a population 1,820. This was larger than what was left behind in each of the parent towns. Not only that, but Stow and Sudbury also stayed close to their post-divestment populations for decades, while Maynard continued to grow. For seventy-five years after the formation of Maynard, its population continued to be larger than the populations of Stow and Sudbury combined.

Chapter 2

MEET THE MAYNARD FAMILY

Given that the town was named after Amory Maynard while he was still alive, there is remarkably little presence of the man today. There is a street, Amory Avenue, but no statue, no school, no park. There is a family crypt and a clock tower (built by his son), but more on those soon. Amory was not running a benevolent company town. The Assabet Manufacturing Company had rules for employees. According to an 1863 document in the possession of the Maynard Historical Society, "The Company will make an effort to employ only those who keep the Sabbath, observe all Regulations, obey their Overseers, preserve carefully the Yarn and other Property in the Mill, and are temperate, skillful and honest." Quitting workers had to give two weeks' notice in order to get their last paycheck but could be fired without notice. Supposedly, there was a 9:00 p.m. curfew, after which workers were expected to be off the streets.

THE MAYNARD FAMILY

In 1846, at the age of forty-two, Amory Maynard moved his wife and three sons to a house in the sparsely settled Assabet River valley so he and his partner, William H. Knight, could dam the Assabet River and build a mill. They started with carpets, in time adding blankets and wool cloth for suits and dresses. Part of their good luck was already being in wool goods when

Amory Maynard, the seventh generation in Massachusetts, bought hundreds of acres of land and water rights to the Assabet River so as to start a woolen mill. He was sixty-seven years old when the town was named after him. *Courtesy of Maynard Historical Society.*

the Civil War embargo cut off Northern cotton mills from access to Southern cotton.

Looking in the ancestral direction, Amory was six generations away from John Maynard, who had decided to leave England for the colonies. (Mary Priest, his wife, was five generations away from John Priest). John Maynard and his young son (also named John) transited the Atlantic, year and ship unknown, but by 1638 were among the initial settlers of Sudbury. The September 1850 census listed Amory Maynard as the head of a Sudbury two-unit household of twenty-four people that included his family, the Adams family, servants and millworkers. Lorenzo was twenty-one; Lucy Ann Davidson (the house servant) was sixteen. They married in October, she having just turned seventeen, and they had their first child thirteen months later. William married Mary Adams, the girl next door, in July 1853. Both marriages lasted more than fifty years and together produced twelve children; nine of those died without having surviving children of their own.

Harlan Maynard, the third son, died at age eighteen; one source specified typhoid fever. Letters in the possession of the Morgan family (descendants of his brother William) portray a spirited young man who was frustrated with small-town life; Assabet Village, as it was known then, had only a few hundred residents. As a teenager, Harlan commuted by train to a private school in Concord, where his classmates included Ralph Waldo Emerson's son.

William had a lesser role in the mill's business affairs than older brother Lorenzo. In the 1860s, William lived in Boston for a while and worked for the Fitchburg Railroad. Tax records from 1871 find him back in Maynard and show Amory, Lorenzo and William with incomes of $9,000, $4,000 and $800, respectively. The combined landownership of the mill, the A&L Maynard Company (a real estate and construction business) and Amory's personal holdings came to 270 acres.

Ten years later, Amory owned a mansion on Beechmont Avenue (now Dartmouth Street) and had extensive landholdings and cash assets of $65,000; Lorenzo also owned a mansion (still standing at 5–7 Dartmouth, stained-glass windows intact) and had cash assets of $35,000. William, at age forty-nine, married and with seven children, was living in a house owned by his father.

Amory Maynard stepped down as mill agent in 1885, shortly after having suffered a stroke. Lorenzo was promoted from superintendent to agent. Lorenzo's son William H. Maynard became superintendent. "Agent" was equivalent to today's title of chief operating officer. Although Amory was the largest shareholder, the post-bankruptcy financial reorganization of the Assabet Manufacturing Company in 1862 had resulted in T.A. Goddard becoming president of the company.

At about the time of Amory's retirement in 1885, his son William moved himself, his wife and the five youngest of their seven children first to Pasadena and then to Los Angeles, at the time a smallish city of twenty-five thousand people. Married daughter Mary Susan and married son Amory both remained in Maynard. Historical accounts state that the move was for William's health (the nature of the illness is unstated). It is plausible that he had tuberculosis, as moving to a hot, dry climate was that era's treatment of choice. But it is also a bit interesting that he moved in the year his brother took over the mill. Regardless, three years later, he was well enough to relocate east, but he chose Worcester over returning to Maynard.

Amory Maynard's death left Lorenzo and William wealthy men. Amory died without leaving a will. Lorenzo was made administrator of the estate, charged with tallying up the net worth, collecting money owed and settling all debts. Although the probate records are silent on the distribution, a good guess is that the estate was divided equally between the two brothers. Unfortunately, neither the probate file nor the state archives have any record of an inventory of Amory Maynard's property or net worth at the time of his death.

Lorenzo continued as agent of the mill and Maynard resident. He personally paid for construction of the clock tower in 1892. William continued to live in Worcester until his death in 1906. At about the same time as the clock tower construction, Lorenzo also paid for the chapel addition and installation of more than a dozen stained-glass windows in the Union Congregational Church, a place of worship that his father had been instrumental in getting started in 1852. Six of the windows were dedicated to Lorenzo's parents and to his deceased daughters.

For complex reasons, including an end of federal protective tariffs in the 1890s, the mill failed in late 1898. It was purchased in 1899 by the American Woolen Company. Lorenzo and his son either resigned or were fired, and then William's son Amory was put in charge as agent. Amory was living in what had been his parents' house near the corner of Main and Nason Streets.

William Maynard was the second son of Amory and Mary. He inherited a sizeable estate upon his father's death. After William died in 1906, his will disposed of an estate estimated at several hundred thousand dollars, equivalent to $7 to 8 million in inflation-adjusted dollars (!) in 2020. *Courtesy of Maynard Historical Society.*

Lorenzo moved to Winchester, where he died in March 1904, a millionaire at a time when an average worker's wages were $500 per year. His son William H. Maynard was his sole surviving heir. An October 1904 newspaper article noted that Lorenzo and five other deceased family members were relocated to a new mausoleum at the Mount Auburn Cemetery, Cambridge—a place where all the "best" people were being buried. Correspondence on file at Mount Auburn confirms that Lorenzo bought the plot #6111, on Crystal Avenue, in April 1903 and immediately ordered the construction of a large mausoleum designed by the renowned Van Amringe Granite Company.

The impressive structure is made of granite, is twenty-four feet tall and had five stained-glass windows (one since destroyed). It was completed in September 1904. Contributing causes for the postmortem move were bad feelings left over from being displaced at the mill, plus the 1902 effort to change the town's name to Assabet.

When Lorenzo's son died in Winchester in 1925, he left no money to his twelve cousins, even though his wife had died years earlier and they had had no children. Instead, his estate of nearly $1 million was divided among his sister-in-law and twenty-three charities, mostly in Winchester. Harlan J. Maynard, a first cousin, challenged the will in court.

Per an account in the *Winchester Star*, William H. Maynard was described by the lawyer representing the cousins as "a man of secret habits and had few friends, but scores of enemies." Claims were made that he was not of sound mind, but rather suffered from "a mental affliction that was inherited through three generations" and that he "thought his servants were trying to poison him." The judge threw all of this out of court.

Amory Maynard, grandson of Amory Maynard, was the last descendant with the family name to live in Maynard. He moved to Cambridge in

Acrimony about the failure of the woolen mill led Lorenzo Maynard to not only move out of town but also contract for an impressive mausoleum at Mount Auburn Cemetery, Cambridge, and have his deceased family members relocated.

1926 and died in 1928. On a mysterious note, his father's will had left money to everyone in the family—except Amory. Mary Susan, his older sister, had four daughters, one of whom, Mary Augusta Peters, married Frank Sanderson. She died in 1947, the last Maynard descendent to live in Maynard. Between deaths and daughters, the family name vanished. There are differently surnamed living descendants via Lessie Louise and Harlan James, but none here.

WHERE DID THE WOOL COME FROM?

The first sheep arrived in New England with the colonists, but they were not of particularly good breeding. Yield was on the order of one pound of wool per year (versus today's ten pounds). Only after the importation of Merino sheep from Spain, starting around 1811, did wool become a serious industry in North America. Ten years later, the U.S. government enacted the Tariff Act of 1823. This included charging a tariff on foreign wool and wool clothing, in order to both raise revenue and protect its nascent wool industry. By 1840, the states of Maine, New Hampshire and Vermont had more sheep than people. The count for Vermont was 1,682,000 sheep to 292,000 people. Most of the land dedicated to sheep grazing has been marginal hill farms vacated by people either moving west or relocating to cities for factory work. We find the mossy remnants of pasture-delineating stone fences throughout New England's woods.

Late spring is when the herds are brought in. Hand shears, later replaced by mechanically powered shears, are used to remove fleece at about three minutes per sheep. Fleece are hot-washed, dried and compressed into bales weighing 260 to 450 pounds each for transport. If the wash and dry steps are skipped, the wool is baled and shipped "in the grease" (meaning the lanolin has not yet been removed).

The value of wool depends on fiber fineness and length. Long fibers with narrow diameter are used for fine-quality clothing, whereas shorter, thicker fibers are used in wool carpets and blankets. Apparently, Maynard's mill was initially buying and processing wool of poor quality because it was producing only carpets. Over time, its output evolved to include blankets and then woven material for clothing. To recap, for the first few years of the mill's existence, wool was either sourced locally or brought by train to the South Action train station and there offloaded into horse-drawn wagons for the final two miles of travel. From 1850 onward, Assabet Village had railroad tracks running directly to the mill.

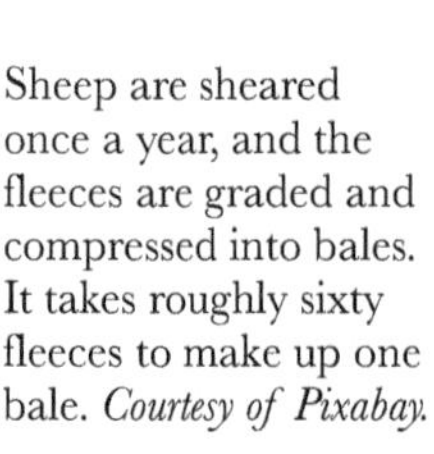

Sheep are sheared once a year, and the fleeces are graded and compressed into bales. It takes roughly sixty fleeces to make up one bale. *Courtesy of Pixabay.*

WHO IS IN THE MAYNARD CRYPT?

According to documents in the collection of the Maynard Historical Society, the remains of twenty-three people are interred in the Maynard family crypt. Surprisingly, this includes but one of Amory and Mary Maynard's three children and only one of their twelve grandchildren.

The crypt, located on the north side of Glenwood Cemetery, is an imposing earth-covered mound with a granite façade facing the road. It was designed and built by Alexander McDonald, a well-known monument architect based in Cambridge, near the Mount Auburn Cemetery. The mound is ninety feet across and about twelve feet tall. The stonework façade is thirty feet across. The ceiling of the crypt has a glass skylight surmounted by an exterior cone of iron grillwork. "Maynard" graces a granite lintel above the entrance. The six-foot-tall double doors are intricately carved Italian marble. One door had been cracked across and repaired.

Inside, there are eight vaults, three each on the left and right sides and two across the back. Each vault was designed to hold three caskets. Above the three on the left is "W. Maynard." Above the two at the back is "A. Maynard." Above the three on the right is "L. Maynard." Some of the vault doors have names and dates incised. In the center of the room is a large marble-topped table.

The crypt was constructed in 1880, while Mary (1805–1886) and Amory (1804–1890) were still alive. They are both interred there, along with their third son, Harlan, who had died in 1861 and was first buried in the cemetery, later relocated to the crypt.

At one point in time, Amory's first son, Lorenzo, along with Lorenzo's wife and their four daughters, were interred in Maynard, but in October 1904, Lorenzo's son arranged to have his six family members moved to a newly constructed mausoleum at Mount Auburn Cemetery, Cambridge, Massachusetts.

William, Amory's second son, and his wife, Mary, are buried at Hope Cemetery, Worcester. They had moved to Worcester in 1888. Of their seven children, Mary S. Peters is the only Amory grandchild buried in Maynard. Also interred there are her husband (Warren Peters), their four daughters (Mary, Irene, Nettie and Bertha) and Mary and Irene's husbands (Frank Sanderson and Leonard Henderson). Mary Sanderson (1874–1947) was the last Maynard descendant to live in Maynard.

William's son Amory, in some accounts referred to as Amory II so as not to be confused with his grandfather, buried his first wife, Ida, and their infant

The Maynard family crypt faces Route 27, at the south end of Glenwood Cemetery. The remains of twenty-two people are interred within.

Chiseled above the lintel are the year 1880 and the Greek letters Alpha and Omega, entwined with a fleur-de-lis cross. Amory died ten years after having this built.

Descendants of Amory and Mary Maynard, through their son William, visited Maynard in 2018.Their tour included the interior of the Maynard family crypt.

daughter, Lola, in the crypt in 1881. But he and his second wife are buried elsewhere—site unknown. The other bodies in residence are descendants of William's son Harlan. Whereas Harlan and his wife, Florence, are not in the crypt, the tally includes six of their children and three of their grandchildren.

Because no descendants live in Maynard, there has been a bit of misconception that there were none. Not true. Amory's son William had seven children. William's daughter Lessie Louise Maynard married Paul Beagary Morgan, of the wealthy and well-known Morgan family of Worcester. Lessie and Paul had five children, who begat children of their own. Another line descends from William's son Harlan to his son John to three daughters. Hence, none of the descendants has Maynard as his or her last name. In 2018, one great-great-granddaughter of Amory and Mary and six great-great-great grandchildren visited Maynard to see the family crypt and peruse parts of the town familiar to their ancestors.

Chapter 3

1871–1921

First Fifty Years

Over this initial fifty-year period, the population increased from 1,820 to 7,080. Maynard officially became a town on April 19, 1871, and had its first town meeting eight days later, selecting men to be selectmen and treasurer (Lorenzo Maynard), a school committee and constables. Also filled were now obsolete posts such as fence viewers and field drivers—the former were paid to identify fences that were not tall and strong enough to contain horses, cattle, sheep and pigs, and the latter were charged with rounding up farm animals that got loose, to be returned to owners only after a fine was paid. Caught animals were held in a pound.

IMMIGRANTS

The U.S. Census Bureau estimated the Maynard 2019 population as 91 percent White, 3 percent Hispanic, 3 percent Asian, 2 percent Black and 1 percent identifying as two or more. The mix was similar for Stow. The Asian-identifying populations of other neighboring towns were higher, with Acton having reached 25 percent. Massachusetts as a whole was 71 percent White, 12 percent Hispanic, 9 percent Black and 7 percent Asian.

Looking at the European immigrants, the English and Scottish were first, then Irish Presbyterians and Catholics, fleeing religious persecution and famines (plural), respectively. A mill payroll list from 1890 shows only

English-, Scottish- or Irish-sounding surnames. However, starting in the 1890s there were waves of immigration to Maynard from Finland, Poland, Russia and Italy, with smaller numbers from Italy, Sweden and Denmark, plus people of the Jewish faith from several European countries. There are no records of any African-born or U.S.-born slaves residing in what would later become Maynard, although there is confirmation of slaves in Concord (fifteen), Sudbury (fourteen), Stow (one) and Acton (one) in a 1754 census.

English

The *Mayflower*'s crossing in 1620 was the first small stone preceding an avalanche of Puritan families leaving England to escape political and religious oppression. This "Great Migration" saw some 20,000 people reach New England between 1628 and 1642. The preponderance of the immigrants were well-to-do gentry and skilled craftsmen. They brought with them wives, children, apprentices and servants. The Massachusetts Bay Colony saw these people arrive in Boston and then move west to settle new towns. Concord was established in 1635 and Sudbury in 1639. The flow of immigrants ceased with the outbreak of civil war in England. With the Puritans fighting for and seizing power in England under Oliver Cromwell, an estimate 7 to 10 percent of men returned to England. Yet the Massachusetts population increased: 8,900 in 1640 became 20,000 by 1660 and 40,000 by 1680. In addition to births in the colony, a goodly portion of the increase was indentured servants, unmarried young men and women from England, Holland and Germany who agreed to work for four to seven years at no pay in return for ship's passage to the New World. England also exported convicts, but that was later and to the southern colonies, which needed plantation workers.

Irish

The first wave of Irish immigrants to the New England colonies were Ulster-area Presbyterians fleeing religious discrimination during 1715 to 1750, many of them Scotch-Irish who had previously relocated from Scotland to northern Ireland for the same reason. Emigration was also sparked by the Irish Famine of 1740–41, which, combining severe cold and drought, killed an estimated 15 to 20 percent of the population. During this era and until around 1790, strict anti-Catholic laws actually prevented the immigration of Catholics to America.

Another famine in 1816, the "Year Without a Summer" (a consequence of a super-volcano eruption in the Pacific), again spiked emigration from Ireland, but the main cause of more than 1 million Catholic Irish taking ships to America was the Irish Potato Famine of 1845–49. Much of the immigration was of young women heading toward jobs in factories or as house servants and of young men heading toward factories or construction jobs, primarily canals and railroads. One account estimated that between 1820 and 1860, the Irish accounted for one-third of all immigrants to the United States. Once situated, these women and men sent money home to bring over relatives, ensuring a flow of immigration well past the end of the century. Roughly one in five people living in Massachusetts can claim Irish ancestry.

Locally, the Scotch-Irish population was never large enough to support a church. With the creation of the woolen mill operation in 1846 by Willian Knight and Amory Maynard, there were jobs for immigrants. By 1850, the population of Irish Catholics had surpassed fifty; a priest traveled from Saxonville (Framingham) or Marlborough twice a year to conduct Mass. In time, the population grew, a church was built on Main Street and a resident pastor was assigned. Within twenty years, the congregation has outgrown in house of worship, leading to the construction and then dedication of St. Bridget's Church at its present location, on Sudbury Street.

Finns and Other Nordic Country Immigrants

Emigrants have many reasons. In the case of Finland, the decisions to leave accelerated during a period of Russification. The Language Manifesto of 1900 made Russian the official language of Finland, and the conscription law of 1901 required all men of Finland to serve in the Russian Imperial Army. Emigration continued during and after the Finnish civil war of 1918, which had followed closely on Finland's declaration of independence from the collapsed Russian empire. Estimates are that more than 400,000 Finns came to the United States or Canada. The first wave headed to Michigan and Minnesota, but later waves, more likely to be political refugees, also went to factory towns in New England, specifically Fitchburg, Worcester, Maynard, Gardner, Quincy and Cape Ann. Maynard's Finnish immigrants started their own churches, co-operative associations, music bands and temperance societies and built commercial saunas.

By 1900, one-fifth of the population of Maynard was of Finnish descent; by 1925, the town's population had doubled after the American Woolen Company had taken over and enlarged the mill and the town was one-third of Finnish descent. Employees at the mill—working sixty-hour weeks—were enjoined to write to family and friends in Finland, promising jobs. According to Roy Helander, a longtime Maynard historian, his father, Edward, arrived in Boston in 1903 speaking no English. Immigration authorities sent him to the train station with instructions pinned to his coat saying which train to be on and where to get off. In time, their children and their children's children gave up speaking Finnish, assimilated and moved away. The co-ops, bands, saunas and churches are gone. Today, the strongest evidence is Finnish names on tombstones at Glenwood Cemetery.

Smaller numbers of people came to Maynard from Denmark and Sweden. They established fraternal organizations (Danish Brotherhood, Scandinavian Brotherhood and others) and held religious services in their own language but did not build their own churches. Assimilation held sway here too.

Poles

According to the centennial history book, a rapid growth of the Polish immigrant population was a result of a strike at the mill in 1911. Employees involved in one aspect of wool processing were mostly Finnish immigrants. After they had unionized and gone on strike, in part protesting against the fifty-four-hour workweek, they were fired and replaced by Poles. The influx of more than six hundred Polish Catholics to Maynard led to services being held in Polish at St. Bridget's Church starting in 1912. Sixteen years later, St. Casimir Roman Catholic Church started services in what had been the powerhouse building of the defunct Concord, Maynard and Hudson Railway (electric trolley). By 1999, the children and grandchildren had assimilated, and no longer speaking Polish, the parish was merged back into St. Bridget Parish; soon after, the building was sold to St. Mary's Indian Orthodox Church of Boston. The Polish immigrants also created the International Co-operative Association in 1911. It lasted twenty years.

Russians

Much like the Poles, Russians were coming to Maynard to work at the mill. Religious services were held at the Congregational Church until St. Mary's Russian Church was dedicated in 1916. The church, with its onion-domed steeple, painted blue, is on Prospect Street. There was an attempt to create a Russian Co-operative Association in 1917, but it collapsed two years later. Russians built a meeting hall building on Powder Mill Road that years later—much enlarged and having done long stints as a restaurant—is now the Elks Lodge. Over time, the descendants of Russian immigrants assimilated, and the church became the Holy Annunciation Orthodox Church, serving all peoples of Orthodox faith. Twice a year since 1978, the church hosts a Bazaar Russe, showcasing Slavic food and displays of cultural items, Orthodox books and icons.

The Holy Annunciation Orthodox Church began as a parish of the Russian Orthodox Church in America. Services were initially conducted in Slavic, changing to English after 1954. *Courtesy of Maynard Historical Society.*

Italians

Much like the Poles and Russians, Italians came for mill jobs. The Italian immigrants forewent creating a church, instead attending St. Bridget's. However, they went big on starting fraternal associations such as Sons of Italy, Italian Citizens' Club, Italian Social Club and St. Anthony's Crusaders. One contribution to Maynard's musical history was the Columbian Mandolin Orchestra, which on summer eves would stroll the streets of Maynard, playing and singing Italian songs. The best-known Italian restaurant was Russo's at 51 Waltham, later site of May Ling, then Oriental Delight; it was torn down circa 2015 for Russo's Village Condominiums.

Jews

Modest numbers of Jews settled in Maynard around the beginnings of the twentieth century. Families by the name of Loewe, Lerer, Gruber and Bachrach operated businesses. Two organizations—the Ednas Israel Society and Maynard Hebrew Society—would invite rabbis from other towns to officiate at services for Jewish holidays. In 1921, MHS founded Rodoff Shalom Synagogue on Acton Street and also started a Jewish Youth Association known as the Double Triangle Club. In the late 1960s, a nascent Jewish community in Acton began to attend services in Maynard, grew and built its own synagogue (with parking!); the shrinking Maynard congregation merged with them in 1980.

Brazilians

Much more recently, but not as obviously, there has been an influx of Portuguese-speaking immigrants from Brazil. For a while, Main Street had a Brazilian goods store and a Brazilian restaurant. St. Bridget Parish holds a weekly Mass in Portuguese. Estimates are that there are 1 million immigrants from Brazil in the United States, with one-fourth of them residing in Massachusetts. Framingham is a nexus, with offshoot clusters in Marlborough, Hudson and Maynard.

THE TOWN CONSIDERED A NAME CHANGE

Maynard almost changed its name thirty-one years after it was founded. Impetus for the name change seemed to be threefold: American Woolen Company, the new owner of the mill complex, wanted the name change; people were still angry that Amory Maynard, the mill founder, had not left a significant gift to the town when he died in 1890; and his son Lorenzo Maynard was accused of mismanaging operations of the mill to the point that it fell into bankruptcy at the end of 1898, costing many millworkers their jobs plus part of their savings, which they had entrusted to the Assabet Manufacturing Company, as there was no bank in town.

A petition filed with the state's Committee on Towns on February 4, 1902, by James B. Lord and a few other townspeople, plus the American Woolen Company, became House Bill No. 903, "An Act to Change the Name of the Town of Maynard." The petition's intent was to change the name of the town to Assabet. The bill called for a majority vote by the legal voters of the

Lorenzo Maynard built this mansion on the hill south of the mill, a short distance away from his father's even larger mansion. An 1889 map shows a reflecting pond in front and a greenhouse on one side. The building is still graced with some of the original stained-glass windows.

town at a special town meeting, with the meeting to be held within ninety days of the passage of the bill. Hearings on the petition were held on March 11, March 18, March 25 (that one in Maynard) and March 28. The March 28, 1902 issue of the *Maynard News* led off with these headlines:

Maynard or What?
Hearing on Change of Name
Arguments For and Against
American Woolen Co. Desires Change

The following paragraphs are excerpts from the article:

The legislative hearing on the petition for a change in the name of the town was continued on Tuesday. The hearing began at the State house, Boston, but after a two hours' session the hearing was continued for one week, the Commonwealth of Massachusetts Committee on Towns deciding to pay a visit to Maynard.

Mr. Murray, representing the petitioners for name change, called Julian Lowe, who stated that he had resided in Maynard about 29 years and had been in the wholesale and retail liquor business about 21 years. He signed the petition for a change of name, and in talking with others has found a decided sentiment existing in favor of the change. He had lost money by the failure of the Assabet Manufacturing Co., and at that time had heard considerable discussion relating to a change of name.

Ashael H. Haynes next appeared for the petitioners. He stated that he had been in the clothing business in Maynard 25 years. He favored the change and believed that the sentiment on town was also that way. Ralph Whitehead believed the sentiment in favor of the change was 3 to 1.

Mr. Murray then called upon James F. Sweeney, who as a life-long resident of Maynard, someone who had known Amory Maynard and knew him as an honest, businesslike man, was nevertheless strongly in favor of the change. Mr. Sweeney spoke of the influence exerted over the voters of the town when the Assabet mills were controlled by the Maynards, intimating that they dared not vote against the mill owners for fear the means of livelihood would be lost.

Mr. Sweeney charged the Maynards with being opposed to the installation of the public water system and the building of the present Nason street schoolhouse. He further stated that when the town was incorporated in 1871, the Maynard family and the Assabet Company owned nearly all the tenements in town. There were no sidewalks, street lights, and but poor educational advantages. He spoke of the lack of a Town Hall, and said that for many years the town had been obliged to pay a high rent for use of Riverside Hall, a building owned by the Maynard family.

He stated that for ten years before its downfall, the Assabet mills had been tottering, and that a few months previous to the failure Lorenzo Maynard, realizing that the end was drawing nigh, signed over property to the amount of $250,000 to protect himself when the crash came. Mr. Sweeney closed with an appeal to the Committee to allow the citizens the privilege of exercising their right to vote on the matter.

Thomas Hillis, in opening for the remonstrants, told of the founding of the original mill, and gave a brief history of Amory Maynard, its founder. He contrasted the size of the place when Amory Maynard first arrived in Assabet valley with the size of the town when Mr. Maynard retired in 1884.

"When Mr. Maynard first came here," said Mr. Hillis, "there were only 12 houses in the place; when he retired from business 1,200 hands were employed at the mills, and the mills had a surplus of $1,000,000 and paid six percent on its capital stock. When the town was incorporated it was given the name of Maynard by the voters, but the honor was not sought by Amory Maynard, and in yielding to the wishes of the townspeople he had made no promises of bequests or memorials in return for the use of his name."

Mr. Hillis added "Because Lorenzo Maynard had failed was no reason why the name should be changed, and that he would show that prior to 1898 no one had ever thought of changing the name of the town."

Mr. M.H. Garfield of the gunpowder mills and Mr. John W. Ogden, superintendent of the trolley, spoke against the petition, as did Mr. Frank H. Harriman of Harriman Bros. Laundry. Mr. Harriman stated that his father had never heard Amory Maynard promising to give anything to the town, and further, that he did not believe in letting the people vote on the question.

Other people well known in Maynard spoke against the petition, among them William B. Case, owner of the dry goods store, Rev. Edwin Smith, retired pastor of the Congregational Church, Abel G. Haynes, John Whitney and Artemas Whitney. In accord was Sidney B. Shattuck, who said that Maynard was good enough for him. He was decidedly against going back to the name "Assabet," as it was an Indian name and he had no use for Indians.

It should be noted that Sweeney's complaints about lack of schools, sidewalks, streetlights and town buildings prior to the incorporation of the town in 1871 were somewhat disingenuously directed toward Amory Maynard. Prior to that year, the land and citizens about the mill were either from Stow (if north of the river) or Sudbury (if south). The main reason the locals petitioned to secede from those parent towns was that they were being taxed but not getting the services they desired.

Furthermore, the newspaper accounts failed to mention that Amory Maynard had donated land for the construction of the Union Congregational Church, and according to the church pastor, he was responsible for many other charitable acts; the paper also did not mention that Lorenzo Maynard had personally paid for construction of the church annex and the clock tower.

There was a reservoir of ill will toward Lorenzo Maynard among the townspeople because of mismanagement of the Assabet Manufacturing Company, leading up to the declaration of bankruptcy at the end of 1898. Highly relevant to why the mill failed, but not mentioned in any of the local historical accounts, was the fact that the U.S. government's Wilson-Gorman Tariff Act of 1894 had ended the protectionist tariffs on imported wool and other goods. This plus the recession that began in 1893 put financial pressure on woolen mills throughout New England, not just in Maynard. Dozens failed. The federal government restored a protective tariff on importation of both raw wool and finished wool fabric in 1897 as part of the Dingley Tariff Act, but it was too late to save the Assabet Manufacturing Company.

"Welcome to Maynard" signs greet people at the borders on major roads. Members of Maynard Community Gardeners maintain flower beds at the bases of some of the signs.

The name change decision rested in the hands of the Commonwealth of Massachusetts Committee on Towns. According to the book *History of Maynard, Massachusetts, 1871–1971*, the Committee on Towns decided on May 2, 1902, by a five to four vote to allow the bill to proceed, but on May 8 the full state legislature killed the bill by a vote of seventy-nine to sixty-nine to not allow a third reading of the bill. There was to be no local vote. Maynard remained Maynard.

THE CLOCK TOWER CLOCK AND 12:10 ON THE TOWN SEAL

Arnold (Skip) Wilson noted, "Until I retired in 2012, I was responsible for winding the clock in the clock tower for almost twenty-five years. This job needs to be done once a week, so I figure since 1892 it's been wound more than six thousand times." Responsibility for this passed from Skip to Leon Tyler.

Lorenzo Maynard arranged for construction of the tower and clock as a memorial to his father, Amory Maynard, cofounder of the mill, who had passed away in 1890. The tower was built from the ground up, with the lower half set between two existing buildings. The red-and-white painted top third is made of wood. The tower's official dedication was held on October 23, 1892. The clock's four faces have always been illuminated by electric lights. While the clock mechanism is original, Digital Equipment Corporation completely renovated the tower in 1980.

The clock is hand-wound, making it one of the few public clocks in New England to run without electric power. Every Monday, an employee climbs the wooden steps to turn cranks that raise weights to provide power to the clock and the bell striker. When fully wound, the weights provide power for eight days.

To visualize the clock, think of it as the grandfather of all grandfather clocks. The room is twelve feet square. Each clock face is nine feet across. The clock mechanism is mounted in a frame about the size of a dining room table, securely bolted to the floor. The pendulum is nine feet long. It extends through a slot in the floor to the room below. Over each week, the weights—suspended by steel cables—slowly descend from the tower to just above the first floor.

Gears behind one of the clock tower's four clock faces turn the minute and hour hands.

Operating directions—on the original piece of paper from 1892—are posted inside the tower. Wilson said that the clock mechanism is so accurate that it is off by only one minute per month at most. Routine maintenance does not require much beyond the occasional oiling. This is good because the company that made the clock, E. Howard & Company, Boston, stopped making tower clocks in 1964.

Lighting the face of the clock is now managed with fluorescent lightbulbs, eight per face. On the special occasions when color is added to the lighting, the method is simple: colored plastic tubes are slipped over the lights. Some years the faces are lit orange around Thanksgiving to coincide with the Maynard High School homecoming football game. Red and green lead up to winter holidays. Blue appeared for the first time in April 2012 to acknowledge World Autism Awareness Day. The tower itself was originally painted in red and white, redone in gray and white from 1942 to 1998 and then reverted to the original white and brick red it sports today.

For many years, Maynard's fifth-grade classes made field trips to the clock tower. Students would ascend the ever-steepening wooden stairs to the cramped room that houses the clock's mechanism to see the pendulum,

The town seal, 1975–present. It was based on Gerard D'Errico's design for the 1971 commemorative coin issued to honor Maynard's centennial.

escarpment, crown gear that drives the four face gears and the triggering mechanism for the bell striker. Sadly, the trips are no more—the school's decision—so students no longer gain firsthand memory of something that helps makes their town different from most.

Maynard's original town seal was one circle inside another. The outer border read Town of Maynard Massachusetts. The inner circle held Incorporated 1871. This seal was replaced in January 1975. Maynard made this change four years after the clock tower was featured on the Town Centennial Coin. Gerard D'Errico won the contest in 1971 for best design for the commemorative coin and was doubly honored when his design was chosen to replace the old town emblem. D'Errico was a graphic artist and design engineer by trade. He served for years in the Maynard Fire Department. He passed away in 2009, survived by his wife, Patricia; son, John; daughter, Marianne; and an extended, multigenerational family.

The motto on the town seal is Progressus Cum Stabilitate, intended to translate from the Latin as "Progress with Stability." D'Errico's centennial coin design read Progressus Cum Stabilitas. *Stabilitate* is the ablative singular form of *stabilitas*. According to Latin scholars, the former is correct when following a preposition such as *cum*. The Town of Maynard is of two minds on this. Official town documents bear the town seal with Stabilitate, as do the newer street signs, but town-owned vehicles with the seal on the door have it as Stabilitas, as does the sign outside the police station. Well, as they say in Latin, *Quicquid* ("Whatever").

The clock on the town seal shows the time as 12:10. Ten minutes after noon is when the fire station used to sound its rooftop horn—audible throughout much of Maynard. Why 12:10 and not noon is shrouded in the mystery of history. Some say the answer is simple: back in the day, when the woolen mill sounded its noon steam whistle to announce lunch break, the fire department decided to offset its own by ten minutes so the two could never be confused. Others say that the person in charge of the daily test would walk up to the train station to get the official time via telegraph, set his watch accordingly and then walk back to the fire house. As the walk to the

A clock face showing the iconic 12:10 time that was incorporated into a revision of the town seal in 1975. Note that four o'clock shown as "IIII" rather than "IV."

fire station, then on Nason Street, was just under ten minutes, the decision was made to be consistent about sounding the horn at 12:10.

According to *A History of the Maynard Fire Department, 1890–1970*, back in 1897, when the fire signal was a battery-triggered release of a striker hitting the school bell (rather than any horn or whistle), budget accounts show that William W. Oliver, who owned a jewelry shop next to the fire station, was being paid twelve dollars per year for managing the daily test—at 12:10. He was the one walking to the train station and back to get the official time. The tradition continued after switching to a steam-whistle at the mill, a diaphone horn at the fire station on Nason Street and then compressed air horns from the roof of the Summer Street fire house. Given that the woolen mill closed in 1950 and the train station followed ten years later, it had to be some combination of nostalgia and inertia that preserved the tradition long after the reasons were gone. The horn suffered a mechanical failure in 2011 and has been silent since. However, the Maynard town seal shows the clock tower clock at 12:10 on town documents, vehicles and street signs.

AUTOMOBILES AND OTHER MEANS OF TRANSPORTATION

The first car that appeared in Maynard in 1899 was a Stanley Steamer owned by Dr. Frank U. Rich. The Harriman brothers, of Harriman Laundry, also went in for steam-powered vehicles, but gas engines were a coming thing. Charles H. Persons purchased the first Ford in town in 1904. This was likely a Model A—eight horsepower, with top speed of twenty-eight miles per hour. Mass production of cars, using methods transferred over from bicycle manufacturing by innovators such as Henry Ford for the Model T, drove prices down. Newspaper ads in 1914 offered Ford Model T cars for $500 ($12,900 adjusted for inflation). By 1910, there were two car dealers in town, repair shops, gas stations, car rental businesses, attempts to control speeding and the first reported accident (a small boy was hit and was bruised but otherwise unharmed). By 1925, the town's annual report numbered 879 motor vehicles in Maynard.

Dr. Frank U. Rich owned the first automobile in Maynard in 1899, a steam-powered vehicle built by the Stanley brothers in Watertown, Massachusetts. Dr. Rich bought a second Stanley in 1903 and a third in 1909. The photo shows him and his daughter, Gertrude, in the 1903 car. *Courtesy of Maynard Historical Society.*

Before cars, there were passenger trains to Boston (1850–1958). Cohabiting with cars, there was an electric trolley system going by the name Concord, Maynard & Hudson Street Railway. It operated from October 1901 to January 1923. In addition to the named towns, there was a spur north to South Acton and, beyond, to West Acton. Trolleys ran every thirty minutes from 6:00 a.m. to 11:00 p.m. It cost a nickel to go from Maynard to the other towns. In addition to the standard passenger cars, either open-sided or closed, CM&H operated custom-built luxury cars for rented use. Think of these as the party limousines of the day. Each of the three cars—the "Concord," the "Maynard" and the "Hudson"—had carpeting, wicker chairs, electric lights and curtained windows. These private cars could be hired for trips and were not limited to CM&H rails. There is a record of a day trip to Woonsocket, Rhode Island!

The trolley barn, located on the west side of where Routes 62 and 117 merge, became the base for the Lovell Bus Lines (1923–54). John Lovell started bus service from Maynard to the South Acton train station. In time, he added bus service to Concord and to Hudson. Eventually, the line was extended west to Clinton and Leominster and east to Waltham and Revere Beach (summers only; a round trip was $1.25). Lovell Bus Lines was sold to Middlesex & Boston Street Railway, which operated trolleys and buses, and later merged with MBTA. Bus service for Maynard dwindled over time, ending in 1972.

Lovell lived a remarkable life. He left school at age nine for factory work, taught himself to read and write in his teens and then alternated factory work with starting his own businesses (with little success at the latter). At sixty-one years old, he found him broke again, with only an old Model T Ford to his name. He went into the taxicab business in Woburn, expanded that to buses and was bought out for $45,000; at age sixty-three, instead of retiring, he started the bus line in Maynard. He stayed involved in daily operations until his death in 1945 at age eighty-seven. Over time, the family sold off parts and then ended their involvement in the business in 1954.

Long before cars and horses, Maynard's annual town reports included assessors' reports, which until 1933 included a horse tally for tax purposes. The maximum was reached in 1899 at 256 horses. A wealthy family of the pre-automobile era might have a carriage house on the property and keep a horse on site or board a horse at a livery stable in town. Richard Parmenter operated a stable off Concord Road. The site of the Fine Arts Theatre was once a livery stable as well. Maynard was also home to a number of urban barns. These were not remnants of working farms, but rather one-horse

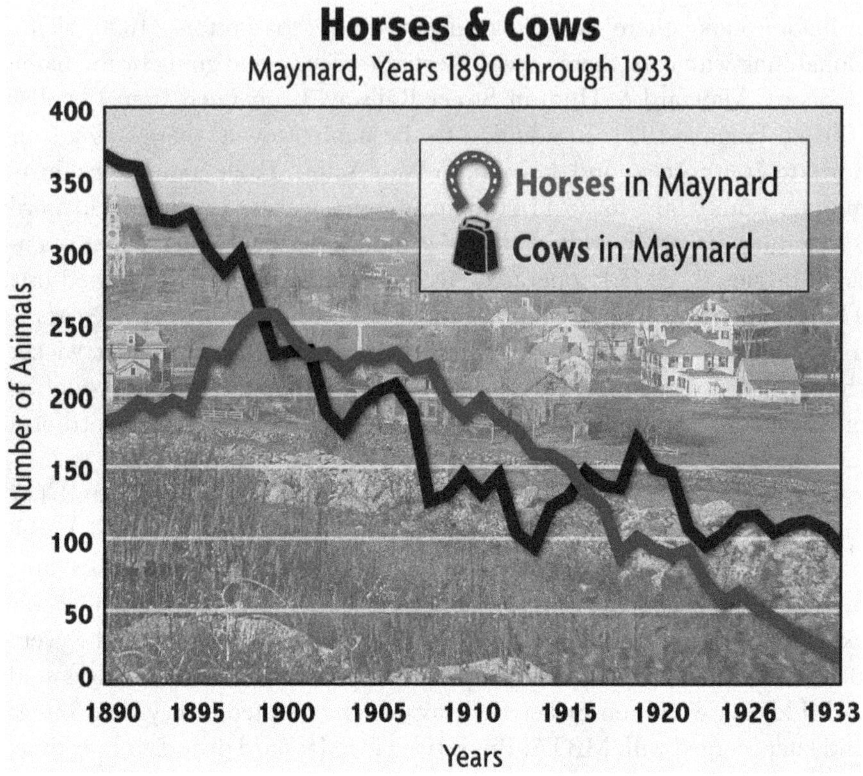

Proportionally, the drop in horse ownership was actually steeper than apparent from the chart, as the number of households doubled between 1900 and 1920, while horses declined from 256 to 120. *Created by Felice Katz.*

barns for people who carted goods about town or to and from the railroad. Larger operations such as Parmenter Farm on the north edge of town were caring for dozens of horses for various businesses.

After 1899, the horse population gradually declined. By 1919, there were only 123 horses and then fewer than 20 when the count stopped in 1933. A few remained. Peter Grigas reminisced about how in the 1950s he and his friends rode their family-owned horses from Maynard to Lake Boon on summer days, stopping at Erikson's Ice Cream on the way back.

Maynard was also a cow town. Records show that more than 350 milk cows resided in Maynard in 1890 and still more than 100 as late as 1933. Living amid manure was the downside of life in Maynard. That peak number of horses would generate about four tons of manure daily, plus an additional two to three tons of urine—mostly at the stables, but a fair bit on

Long after steamboat service on the Assabet ended, the *Princess* serviced the landing near the train station, taking people to and from docks around Lake Boon. This photo is from 1926. *Courtesy of Maynard Historical Society.*

the roads. The cows would have added another ton of manure, albeit not scattered about town, but still contributing to the olfactory ambiance. And don't even start to think about the hundreds of pigs! Maynard was a horse town, a cow town, a pig town and a fly town!

Lastly, steamboats operated on the Assabet River from 1906 to 1914, offering transportation from a dock at the rear of the trolley headquarters to Whitman's crossing, near Lake Boon. Transportation started with one boat, named *Queen*, but in time added *Gertrude* and *Teddy*. On weekends, boats departed hourly. The short walk to Lake Boon brought people to a dock where the *Princess* would take them to docks scattered around to lake, providing access to summer cottages, clubhouses, restaurants and drinking establishments.

And the Band(s) Played On

Music has been an essential part of Maynard before Maynard was Maynard. The town's inaugural parade featured the Eagle Cornet Band of Iola Lodge and the Amateur Brass Band. The Maynard Brass Band came into being in 1875, reorganized in 1884 as the Maynard Military Band. The Finnish

Imatra Band formed in 1898 and the Finnish National Band in 1910. Various fife and drum corps, choral groups and glee clubs also entertained Maynard during the first half of the twentieth century.

In 1904, Abel Haynes donated a bandstand to the Maynard Military Band. It stood at the corner of Walnut and Main Streets and was illuminated by electric lights, with electricity courtesy of the woolen mill. Concerts were Wednesday evenings, from June through Labor Day. Hundreds of people would stand (or sit, if they brought chairs) to listen to the music. This was not as traffic-disruptive as one might think, as there were fewer than a dozen cars in all of Maynard. However, the crowd did have to make way periodically for the electric trolley. Sadly, a feud erupted over which bands would use the bandstand. While MMB claimed that it "owned" the bandstand, it stood on town property. The town called for sharing. The bandstand was moved on June 4, 1915, to a yard on Acton Street until the dispute was resolved. It never returned. A fieldstone bandstand was constructed in Crowe Park in 1939 but was torn down in the 1990s.

The Maynard school system offers many opportunities for the musically inclined. Concert Band, Pep/Marching Band and Concert Chorus are credit-earning courses, while Wind Ensemble, Jazz Band, Honors Chorus and A Capella Choir are non-credit electives. The school functions are supported in part by the Maynard Music Association.

In addition to Maynard's own bands, choruses and glee clubs, organizations in town frequently brought in orchestras for dances. The historical society has in its collection posters for dance marathons, masked balls and even "Battle of Music" events, at which two orchestras would play and attendees would vote for the best.

At times, there were problems. On November 14, 1913, the weekly local newspaper, the *Maynard News*, carried this item: "At the Selectmen's meeting Wednesday evening, it was decided that the objectional dances which have been indulged in in the dance halls in this village must be stopped. All parties holding dances in the future will be notified that these objectionable and so-called animal dances are prohibited and must not be permitted in any dance hall in this municipality…in this action for a cleaner and better Maynard."

The "Animal Dance" craze was directly related to the popularity of ragtime music, derived from African American traditions, with a syncopated beat. Maynard was not alone in prohibiting provocative dances. In 1912, New York City placed the Grizzly Bear under a "social ban," along with other "huggly-wiggly dances" like the Turkey Trot, Texas Tommy and the Boston Dip.

The Maynard Community Band, assembled in Memorial Park. *Courtesy of Jonathan Daisy.*

Once upon a time, gods and demigods of rock-and-roll walked the streets of Maynard. It was the '70s. Aerosmith, the Talking Heads, The Cars, Tommy Bolin Band, Johnny Barnes, Thundertrain and more all recorded at the Great Northern Studio (aka Northern Studio, Northern Recording Studio, Northern Sound or Northern Lights Recording Studio), upstairs at 63 Main Street. The studio was started by Peter Casperson and Bob Runstein, both out of Boston. Life at the studio must have been interesting. Take, for example, this comment from a forum post: "The first time I ever saw a 'beer machine' [soda machine stocked with cans of beer] was at Northern Sound in Maynard....I thought it was the coolest thing in the world!!!"

Today, the Maynard Community Band performs in Memorial Park. The band—all volunteer—was started in 1947. It was brought together when Finnish immigrant Louis Koski—a professional conductor and composer—invited musicians together from the Maynard Military, Imatra and National Bands. In time, Koski turned over the reins to Ilmari Junno, who in turn turned them over to Alexander DeGrappo, who in turn turned them over to Michael Karpeichik in 2003. Musicians from surrounding towns are welcomed. The band plays a wide repertoire, focusing on quality concert music, standard band repertoire and modern compositions. A "Star Wars" medley is always a crowd pleaser. Performances include ten to twelve annual outdoor summer concerts, as well as spring and fall performances, ending with a Holiday Christmas concert at The Sanctuary (formerly the Congregational Church) in mid-December.

BEFORE NATIONAL PROHIBITION

In 1911, at the March town meeting, Maynard voted to stay "wet" on the issue of local option prohibition, meaning that the town would continue to license saloons and liquor stores to operate legally, with the vote tally at 467 to 340. Maynard remained wet through 1914 but voted itself "dry"—suspending the sale of alcohol—by a tally of 521 to 519 in 1915.

Hudson was going through similar gyrations. Ten years earlier, the votes were consistently pro-licensing. Hudson voted itself dry in 1910, wet in 1911 and then back to dry in 1912. Just before national Prohibition went into effect in 1920, the majority of towns in Massachusetts were already dry, while Maynard was still wet.

Perusal of the library's microfilm of the March 9, 1900 edition of the *Maynard News* found a large front-page advertisement "WHY MAYNARD SHOULD HAVE LICENSES." Among the arguments: "License means more business, more money [saloons paid taxes], less drunkenness, a better standing in the commercial world and the life of a progressive town, while no-license means stagnation, dives, kitchen barrooms, vile liquors, more policemen, higher taxes and no satisfaction."

Wet did not always win. The year 1903 saw a dry vote in Maynard by 379 to 301 after nine straight years of pro-wet voting. The 1904 vote stayed dry, perhaps influenced by an impassioned pre-vote letter in the newspaper reading in part:

> *Maynard as it is today, or Maynard as it was a year ago; Maynard with the streets clear of the hideous sight of a reeling drunkard, or Maynard with the police records showing as many as seven and eight arrests in one day, as was often the case not more than a year ago; Maynard with its midnight street brawls and saloon carousals resulting in the sight of human gore spilled on the streets and in the saloon…or Maynard as it stands today a clean and respectable town with these disreputable and horrible conditions wiped out.*

Regardless, the 1905 vote reverted to wet by 451 to 361. The newspaper mentioned that the town intended to grant five licenses to sell liquor.

Anti-alcohol sentiments have had a long, long history in America. Sermons and speechifying against the evils of alcohol waxed during the early 1800s, waned with the Civil War and then built strength again with the Industrial Revolution's growth of cities, as factory jobs put more cash and opportunity

Thirsty men hoping for a ride to Marlboro to buy beer. Prior to national Prohibition, towns in Massachusetts voted themselves wet or dry every year. *Drawing by Bruce Davidson.*

to drink into the hands of workingmen than farm labor ever had. Saloons were a place to stop for a shot or two (or three or four) before heading home. Married men might find their wives and children at the factory gate at the end of payday, hoping to shame their husbands into handing over money for rent, groceries and such before their husbands made it to the saloons and pool halls. Collectively, all the anti-alcohol activity led to Prohibition going into effect nationwide. Prohibition proved to be wildly unpopular and was repealed in 1933. Localities could still vote themselves dry. Lincoln, Weston and Harvard were still dry as late as 2007 but are now all wet.

Marijuana

The legalization of selling recreational marijuana in the Commonwealth of Massachusetts was a consequence of a referendum voted on in November 2016. This had followed voter approval of "medical" marijuana in 2012, allowing people with cancer, glaucoma and other medical conditions to receive a physician-approved registration card and make purchases at a dispensary. One opened in Acton, but none opened in Maynard. After legalization of recreational marijuana, the first two stores in the state opened in November 2018. As of December 2019, there were thirty-three facilities, the closest one to Maynard being in Hudson; two or three are planning to open in Maynard in 2021. As an interesting echo of town-by-town prohibition of alcohol sales more than one hundred years ago, the neighboring towns of Acton, Concord, Stow and Sudbury have at least initially banned the sale of recreational marijuana. This does not preclude those Massachusetts residents from growing their own, but if they want to bypass growing, harvesting, drying, trimming and aging, residents will have to travel to Maynard or elsewhere to make their purchases.

Chapter 4
A RIVER AND A RAILROAD

The river was the reason for the town, but the railroad was the making of the town. Rivers with enough volume and vertical drop can be dammed to power timber and grain-grinding mills, which operate seasonally. With the right topography, a large enough millpond can be created to provide year-round water power. But without a railroad to bring raw material in and finished goods out, the Industrial Revolution would never have reached Maynard. The woolen mill started operations in 1847. A railroad connecting Boston to Fitchburg opened in 1845. A branch from Acton through Maynard to Hudson opened in 1850.

POWERING THE WOOLEN MILL

Deep in the bowels of Mill & Main, there is a space where an antiquated monster once sat—the turbine that converted water power to electrical power. This machine was the last of several generations of hydropower-generating engineering in the mill.

Hydropower is all about high school algebra. Vertical drop in feet multiplied by flow in gallons per minute divided by 10,000 equals kilowatts, and kilowatts multiplied by 1.34 equals horsepower. For the metric-minded, vertical drop in meters multiplied by flow in liters per second multiplied by 9.81 divided by 1,000 also equals kilowatts. By this math, ten gallons of water dropping one hundred feet yields the same power as one hundred gallons of water falling ten feet.

Wherever greater vertical drop allowed, water was led over the top of the wheel to pull blades downward by force of gravity. This style, referred to as "overshot," traditionally captured 50 to 70 percent of available energy. By the 1830s, wheels would have had wooden blades, rims and spokes attached to iron hubs and axles. Late in the 1800s, the Fitz Waterwheel Company was selling all-steel water wheels, with the advantages of nearly 90 percent efficiency plus resistance to icing in winter.

Back to Maynard, or what at the time was known as Assabet Village. Construction of the Ben Smith Dam, the millpond and the canal between the two in 1846–47 resulted in a large year-round water reserve at an altitude above sea level of 175 feet. Outflow from the waterworks would have reentered Assabet River below the mill at 155 feet. Flow rate through the system is not known, nor the design, but a good guess is two overshot wheels with a combined flow of up to 100 cubic feet of water per second (cfs). Keep in

The Ben Smith Dam, so named because it was built on land sold by Ben Smith to Amory Maynard and William Knight, holds back miles of water, used now for boating and fishing. Year-round, average flow over the top of the dam is about 500,000 gallons per hour but can drop to 5 percent of that in summer drought.

mind that water power production was never around the clock. Flow through the mill was stopped at the end of the workday to back up as much water as possible in the millpond for the next day.

Water power production in the woolen mill's early years was equivalent to about fifty horsepower. As Maynard's mill operations grew, water power was supplemented by coal-fueled steam power, hence all the historic images with smokestacks.

At some point, the water wheel complex was replaced by a turbine. Turbines are much more compact than wheels. Water drops down through a progressively narrowing pipe. This water, now under high pressure, jets into the turbine chamber at high speed, spins the turbine blades and exits out the bottom.

According to an article in the March 14, 1902 issue of the *Maynard News*, the switch to electric power included the installation of coal-powered engines directly connected to electric generators. From this time forward, hydropower was clearly a minor portion of total energy production. Records show, however, that a hydroturbine was still being used to generate electricity from 1902 to 1968. Digital Equipment Corporation refurbished the hydroelectric power plant in 1983 and ran it until 1992. Clock Tower Place petitioned in 2002 to surrender electricity generating rights, describing the retired turbine as having a pass-through of 128 cfs and production of 125 kilowatts of energy. Today, the turbine is retired, the smokestack is merely a support for cellphone antennae and all of the kilowatt hours used to power the mill complex by day and light up the windows by night are wired in from elsewhere.

A RAILROAD TOWN

The mills in what are now Maynard, Stow, Hudson and Marlborough were serviced by freight trains running on a 12.4-mile-long spur that branched southwest from the Boston–Fitchburg line. The branch point was east of what is now the South Acton train station. Amory Maynard, one of the prime movers in securing the right of way, was given in reward a lifetime free pass. In Assabet Village, he was appointed station agent.

These were steam-powered trains. Burning coal heated water to create high-pressure steam, which was then piped to the pistons to provide power. Each exhaust stroke from the pistons pushed the depleted steam out the

This 1912 image of the railroad station, taken from a postcard, shows the Main Street side. The buildings glimpsed behind still grace Railroad Street. After it was demolished, a modest brick building was erected on the site as an auto service station. *Courtesy of Maynard Historical Society.*

smokestack, mingled with smoke, sparks and cinders from the firebox. The tender, behind the engine, would carry about three tons of water and one ton of coal.

The spur (freight and passenger) was operated to Hudson by July 1850 and extended to Marlborough in 1855. The worst accident involving Maynard residents occurred on Sunday evening, November 26, 1905. Scores of people were returning to Maynard after weekend excursions to Boston. This local-stops train was running late, so warning flares were left by the tracks as the train left Lincoln. Behind, on the same track, was the Montreal Express. The engineer of the Express testified that he had seen the flares and slowed but was still traveling so fast that when the rear of the preceding train came into view, even using emergency brakes could not achieve a stop in time. Newspaper accounts described the accident as occurring at 8:15 p.m., resulting in seventeen dead and twenty-five to thirty seriously injured. The dead included nine Maynard residents. The death toll would have been higher except for railroad employees and passengers from both train braving the smoke and fire and risk of a boiler explosion to extract the trapped and wounded.

In a much smaller incident, the last two cars of a passenger train derailed in Maynard on Easter Sunday, April 16, 1911, causing numerous injuries but no fatalities. By that time, the original Fitchburg Railroad Company had been taken over by the Boston & Maine Railroad. Passenger service to Marlborough ended in 1932, ended for Hudson and Stow in 1939 and finally ended for Maynard on May 16, 1958. Maynard's passenger station, built circa 1900, was demolished in 1960. Freight service had diminished over the years, dramatically dropping off when the American Woolen Company ceased operations in 1950.

The last freight run was some time in the late 1970s. The line itself was officially declared abandoned in 1979. By then, trees were growing between the rails. A few older residents of Maynard can remember walking the trestle over the river—quite a daring act, as there were no railings and the Assabet River was dozens of feet below. The railroad right of way from South Acton to Marlborough became the Assabet River Rail Trail.

ASSABET RIVER: FROM TRASHED TO TREASURED

What's in a Name

As for how "Ass-a-bet" came to be the name of a river, it's a mystery. Etymology is the study of the history of words, their origins and how their form and meaning have changed over time. Our problem here is that various nineteenth-century histories attribute the origins to a Native American name, but if that is true, it would have been from the Nipmuc dialect of the Algonquian family of Indian languages. There is no resource to pursue this theory back to an original source. Supposed translations suggest "the reedy place," "the miry place" or "the backward flowing river place." A mire—like a marsh or bog—is more permanent than a temporally fleeting muddy place. "Backward flowing" is a reach. On infrequent occasions, the Sudbury River upstream from the junction of the Sudbury and Assabet flows backward. This happens after heavy rain, and it happens because water from the steeper Assabet reaches the junction sooner than water from the flatter Sudbury. Place names are rarely given for rare events, so this theory feels unlikely.

When Concord was established in 1635, the land—purchased from Native Americans—was originally referred to as Musketaquid for "grassy plain"; perhaps it also indicated the river, as another history translates Musketaquid as "reedy river." Upstream, the river forked at Egg Rock. River exploration tends to start at a river's mouth and work upstream, with naming following. At a major branching, a decision is needed—is one the river and the other a tributary? Or is it better to think of the situation as two branches of the same river? Concord maps from 1753 to as late as 1835 refer to the north branch (now the Assabet) as North River or, on some maps, Concord NR. Some of those maps identify the south branch as the Concord River rather than the Sudbury River.

In Stow, established in 1683, the river's name was in flux, with various maps and documents reading Asibeth, Assabath, Elsabath, Elsibeth, Elizabeth, Assabett, Assabet and more. One map even had it as Stow River. There was a consensus in 1830 that Elizabeth Brook flowed into Elizabeth River into Concord River, but by 1856, when Middlesex County was being remapped in great detail, it was Assabet Brook flowing into the Assabet River, with the pre-Maynard community identified as Assabet Village. (Nowadays it is Elizabeth Brook into Assabet River.) There is a well-known circa 1846 quote from author and Concord resident Nathaniel Hawthorne that, when cited now, usually has the "Assabet" spelling, but what he actually wrote was, "Rowing our boat against the current, between wide meadows, we turn aside into the Assabeth. A more lovely stream than this, for a mile above its junction with the Concord, has never flowed on earth."

A "Worked" River

Given its modest length and modest volume, the Assabet was an extremely "worked" river, meaning that little remains of its original natural state. Seven towns draw their well water from within the Assabet valley watershed and discharge treated wastewater into the river. From the headwaters in Westborough, elevation 320 feet, where a dam ensures less flow in times of flood and more flow in times of drought, to the conflux thirty-one miles and 210 feet lower in elevation where it merges with the Sudbury River to become the Concord River, the Assabet had historically powered eight mills, had its high-water rampages hobbled by flood-control dams, suffered channeling between restraining walls through the center of Hudson and Maynard, lost water to our various usages and gained water back from wastewater treatment facilities.

Henry David Thoreau's journal entry in 1859 noted, "So completely emasculated and demoralized is our river that it is even made to observe the Christian Sabbath…for then the river runs lowest owing to the factory and mill gates being shut. Not only the operatives make the Sunday a day of rest but the river too, to some extent, so that the very fishes feel the influence…of man's religion." His point here is that natural flow was stopped at the end of Saturday's workday so as to back up as much water as possible before work started again Monday morning.

The Assabet was also an extremely polluted river. As Ann Zwinger wrote in *A Conscious Stillness* (1982), "the reach above the Powder Mill Dam is closed by joint action of the Maynard and Acton boards of health"; she added that "the river smell is nauseating, reeking like an unpumped-out campground outhouse times ten." Others described the Assabet as the "Cesspool of

Massachusetts." By then, the issue was no longer industrial pollution left over from the mills that had dotted the Assabet River and its tributaries. Rather, the smells emanated from rotting of bacteria, algae and water plants such as duckweed—the consequence of eutrophic growth promoted by the excesses of phosphorus and nitrogen entering the water from wastewater treatment plants. Surface water runoff of fertilizer from farms, golf courses and lawns also contributed unwanted nutrients, as did untreated storm water from roads and parking lots. Today, all treatment plants comply with a much lower phosphorus discharge. Midsummer phosphorus content in the river has been reduced from 0.4–0.8 milligrams per liter to about 0.1 milligrams per liter. A target is to get below 0.025 milligrams per liter. Over time, the water quality will continue to improve.

All this focus on plant growth is not to say that local rivers had not suffered from industrial insult. Back in the day, wool arrived in Maynard unwashed. Cleaning it at the factory meant that all the lanolin, dirt, urine and feces

During the dirty river decades, it was common for people to dispose of old car tires by tossing them off the Walnut Street bridge (*pictured*) or from the Elks Lodge parking lot. Recent river cleanups yield only modest amounts of trash and few tires. *Courtesy of Maynard Historical Society.*

matted into the fleece ended up in the river, along with the chemical dyes and whatever else. Children frolicked in the river behind the Main Street School (where town hall is now), but not downstream of the mill.

Solid waste trash also contributed to the Assabet's lack of ambiance. In Maynard alone, decades of annual river cleanups organized by the Organization for the Assabet, Sudbury and Concord Rivers (OARS) have removed more than one thousand car and truck tires, tons of metal scrap and hundreds upon hundreds of pounds of broken glass. Intact glass bottles from fifty to sixty years ago have come out of the river. Ditto televisions, bicycles, shopping carts, beer cans and more. A saving grace here is that cleaning up the river appears contagious, so that each year less new trash goes into the river.

A Flooded River

Imagine yourself standing facing upstream on the middle of the Main Street bridge. The river at this point is barely fifty feet wide. The watershed draining into this narrow gap is 114 square miles in area. The historic floods described here were usually the result of a one-two punch: one storm system or winter thaw to saturate the ground and raise the river, followed closely by a second storm dumping huge amounts of rain. A not-impossible storm of four inches of rain would mean 8 billion gallons of water headed your way.

Historical records show that about every ten to fifteen years or so, either a fall hurricane or spring rains flood the Assabet. The U.S. Geological Survey maintains a gauge situated upstream from the Waltham Street bridge. It measures depth and flow-rate in cubic feet per second (cfs). Officially, Maynard is in "flood" when depth reaches 5 feet and volume 1,000 cfs. At this stage, the river is still entirely within its banks but moving fast; 6 feet means a volume of 1,700 cfs, 7 feet means 2,400 cfs, 8 feet means 3,400 cfs and 9 feet means 4,400 cfs. Since the USGS started keeping records in 1942, only five floods have exceeded 7 feet.

According to the National Weather Service, "The 1927 hurricane season brought a tropical storm that swept northward across western New England on Nov. 3–4, 1927. As its warm, humid air rose over the mountains and hills, torrential rains fell, causing severe flooding over extensive areas in virtually all of northern New England." Locally, the November 11, 1927 issue of the *Maynard News* reported water flooding the mill buildings. The existing Waltham Street bridge had been built in 1840 and then widened to add an

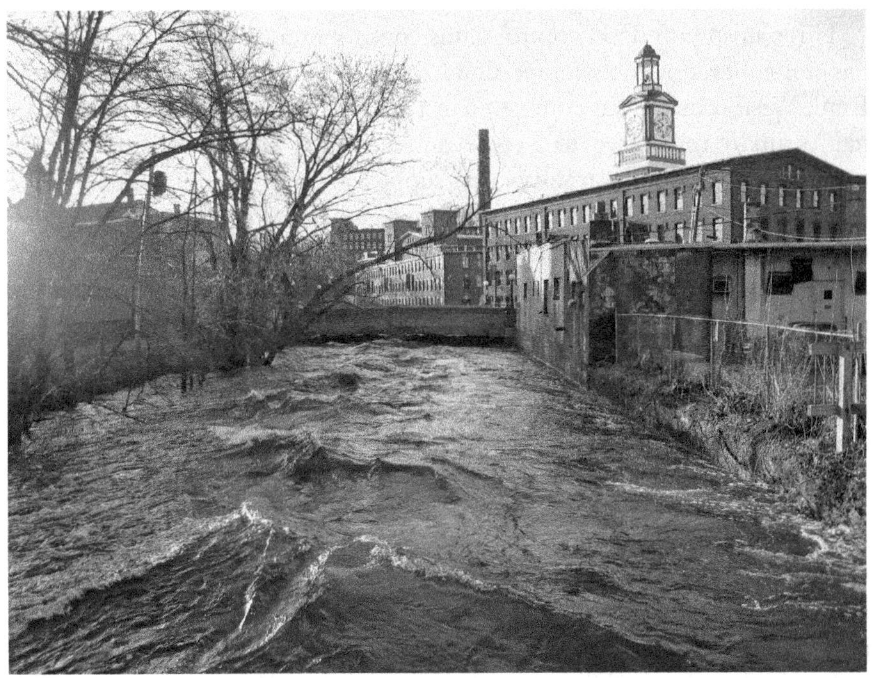

In March 2010, after weeks of intense rain, water depth at the U.S. Geological Service gauge reached 7.1 feet and a volume of 2,500 cubic feet per second (1.6 billion gallons per day). The water level was just inches below the Main Street bridge.

electric trolley track and sidewalk circa 1900. It was severely damaged by the flood. The replacement bridge was dated 1928; replacement of that bridge was completed in 2013.

In 1955, Hurricane Diane dropped more than twelve inches of rain on eastern Massachusetts in just three days. High water crested at 8.94 feet, flooding Main Street, mill buildings and Route 62 on the east side of town. Lesser floods hit Maynard in 1968, 1979, 1987 and 2010. The first of these four put water over the retaining wall between the river and the mill complex, necessitating frantic sandbagging and pumping to save Digital Electronic Corporation. One-time DEC employee Jack MacKeen said, "I have a clear mental picture of Ken Olsen [president of Digital Electronic Corporation] in his suit and rubber boots, helping place sandbags between the buildings." Afterward, DEC had the river retaining wall on its side of the river built higher. The wall kept the river out of the mill during the equally high flood of January 1979, but the lower end of Walnut Street was again under water.

Three upstream flood-control dams contribute to the fact that Maynard has not suffered a catastrophic flood since 1955. The George H. Nichols Dam, Westborough, was completed in 1968. Its reservoir of a bit more than half a square mile serves as a recreational boating and fishing site. It holds back high water and also serves as a supply of water for the Assabet River in times of drought. Tyler Dam, Marlborough, does not obstruct any flow during normal river conditions but rather backs water into an otherwise swampy impoundment area during high water. The third major holdback is the Delaney Complex, on Elizabeth Brook, completed in 1971.

A Recreational River

The Assabet River in Maynard is bisected by the Ben Smith Dam. This structure is 9.5 feet tall and 170 feet wide and was built in 1847 to hold back water for Maynard's woolen mill operations. Behind it, the Assabet is backed up for five miles, almost to the Gleasondale Dam. Ice House Landing offers parking and, starting in 2017, a kayak/canoe launch dock onto this quiet water. At the Maynard/Stow border, where White Pond Road bridges the river, it is possible to launch small trailered boats. Westward, the south shore is bordered by Track Road and the Assabet River National Wildlife Refuge; the north shore is bordered by Gardner Hill Town Forest, Stow.

Downstream from the dam, the river flows rapidly through the center of Maynard. In passing, it is worth noting that much of downtown Maynard is actually an island! The river and canal split above the Ben Smith Dam. The canal waters lead to the millpond, while the river flows on the north side of Main Street. Discharge from the pond rejoin the river east of the mill complex, near the Walnut Street Bridge.

There are only a few locations within Maynard that offer good viewing of the river. John J. Tobin Riverfront Park, by the Rail Trail bridge, is a small greenspace with benches facing the river. Six road bridges provide vantages: Route 62/117, Mill, Florida, Main, Walnut and Waltham. A longish stretch of boring (walled) river can be viewed from the Walnut Street sidewalk. For the adventuresome, the Blue/Green Trail, also known as the Assabet River Walk, starts at the end of Colbert Avenue and extends east into Acton, roughly parallel to and providing woodland views of the river.

Wildlife sightings in town and upstream of the dam include great blue herons, stalking the shallows for fish, crayfish and frogs. Beaver and muskrat use the river as their roadway, the former taking down small trees for food

Beaver are common along the Assabet River. Beaver lodges are sited on the shore every mile or so, and tree damage is widespread. The photo shows the gnawing and chewing teeth. The dark, outward-facing enamel is orange in color and harder than the white dentin behind it, so the gnawing teeth, which grow continually, are self-sharpening.

and at times gnawing on large trees just to keep their ever-growing teeth short and sharp. Mute swans raise families on the still waters upstream of the dam, the same waters populated by eastern painted turtles, which bask in the sun to warm up, swim around eating plants and water insects, bask more, eat more and then sink to the bottom to sleep. Sightings of snapping turtles are rare except for in June, when females are leaving ponds and rivers to find places to lay eggs. These wanderings at times end up in the newspaper police reports. Volunteer efforts do a fairly good job of managing water chestnut, an invasive water plant that, if uncontrolled, can completely cover the water surface. Shorelines of the Assabet River have extensive growths of purple loosestrife, another invasive.

As for fishing, the Assabet River is less of a river and more of a series of dam-created shallow lakes. The fish population is dominated by species that tolerate warm water: bluegill and other "sunfish," white sucker, largemouth bass, eel, carp, catfish, pickerel and more. There are on occasion fish kill events that can leave the surface and shores of the river upstream of the

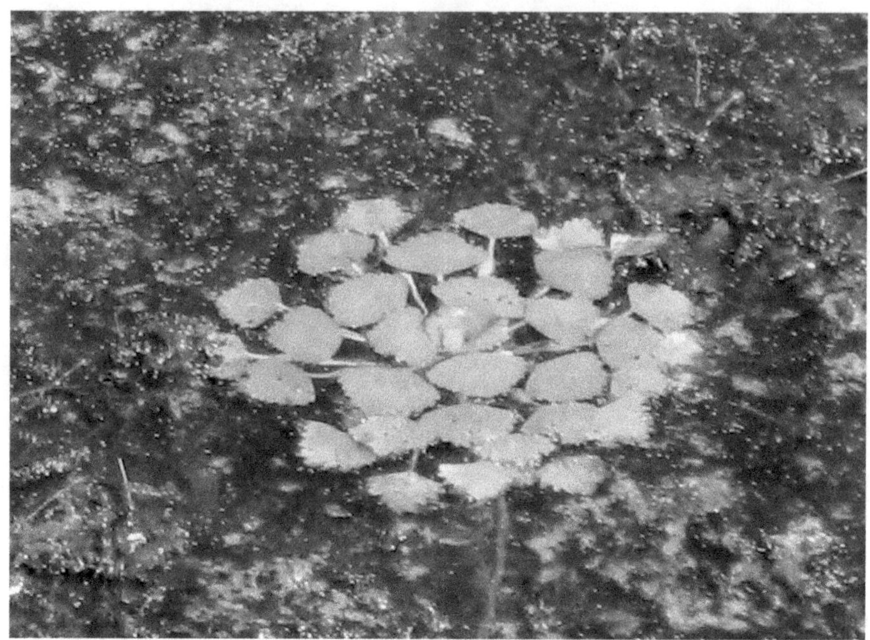

Water chestnut (*Trapa natans*) is an invasive species annual water plant. Stems grow upward from seeds resting on the bottom, and then leaves spread across the surface. It was introduced in eastern Massachusetts in the 1870s. Unchecked, it almost completely covers water surfaces, making boating, swimming and fishing impossible. Control on the Assabet River is by volunteers in boats, pulling up the plants by hand before seeds mature and drop.

dam littered with hundreds, nay, thousands of dead fish. Causes are either low water oxygen or high water temperatures. Past industrial pollution contaminated the Assabet River (and Puffer Pond, in the wildlife refuge) with mercury and other toxins. Children younger than twelve years and women who are pregnant or breast feeding should not consume any fish caught in the river or the millpond. Others should limit consumption to two meals per month. Officially, the Assabet River is not rated clean enough for swimming.

There was a feasibility study by the U.S. Army Core of Engineers in 2010 on removing all the dams on the river and dredging hundreds of thousands of cubic yards of sediment. Consequences would include the loss of the millpond, as water would no longer be diverted through the canal, and the conversion of the boatable upstream stretch to a river that most of the time would be twenty-five to fifty feet wide and about one foot deep. This is not in any federal or state budget, as it's just a concept for now.

Chapter 5
1921–1971

Second Fifty Years

Unlike neighboring towns, Maynard had reached more than half its current population by 1921 (Acton, by comparison, reached only one-tenth) and was already a mature town as far as roads and a downtown business section. The population increased from 7,080 to 10,000 in this fifty-year period, most of that in new houses in the northwest side of town. The two largest changes to Maynard were the land seizure by the U.S. Army during World War II and the end of the woolen mill in 1950.

MONEY, MONEY, MONEY

Approaching Maynard's 150th anniversary, the town is served by Middlesex Bank and Citizens Bank. Of course, for many people their cellphone is their bank, but you don't get a safe deposit box or free lollipops with that.

The first mention of banking services in Maynard predates 1900. The Assabet Manufacturing Company, under management by Lorenzo Maynard, allowed employees and citizens of Maynard to have money in interest-earning savings accounts; employees earned 5 percent and non-employees 4 percent. At the time the company declared bankruptcy on December 31, 1898, deposits were $132,000. According to the centennial history book, on August 12, 1899, assignees managing the distribution of mill assets paid the depositors 25 percent and then, on February 23, 1900 (after the purchase by the American Woolen Company), an additional 35 percent. (Different accounts of the event say that employees got either a combined 55 percent or 66⅔ percent.) There were rumors at the time that the mill owners and Maynard family had diverted funds before the bankruptcy and that Lorenzo Maynard signed over mill property estimated at $250,000 to protect himself when the crash came. Such was the animosity that a few years later there was a failed attempt to change the name of the town to Assabet.

Starting in 1898, the Hudson Cooperative Bank (established in 1885) had an agent, not a branch, in Maynard. People could make mortgage payments and deposit savings with George Salisbury, who was station agent at the train station. This made sense because he could take the train to Hudson. George was succeeded by Charles H. Persons (his main job was as a musical instrument salesman) and then by Frank E. Sanderson, who served as bank agent at his store. Frank is better known to Maynard history as the town clerk from 1913 to 1948 and also for being entombed in the Maynard family crypt with his wife, Mary Augusta (Peters) Sanderson (1874–1947), the great-granddaughter of Amory and Mary Maynard, last descendant to live in Maynard.

Assabet Institution for Savings, the first bank in Maynard, opened on April 29, 1904. Its first physical location was in the Riverside Block—the building was later home to Gruber Bros. Furniture. Then an impressive brick building was constructed at 17 Nason Street in 1929, and the bank moved there in January 1930. It survived the Great Depression, morphed into Assabet Savings Bank and in time was acquired by Middlesex Savings Bank.

The U.S. Postal Savings System was operated by the U.S. Post Office from 1911 to 1967. These savings accounts were popular during the Great Depression because they were backed by "the full faith and credit of the United States Government." President Roosevelt's creation of the Federal Deposit Insurance Corporation in 1933 provided security for commercial banks, lessening the attractiveness of postal savings.

Maynard Trust Company began operations in 1913 as Maynard's second bank. The MTC building at 75 Main Street, under a statuary eagle and the founding date, opened for business in 1926. MTC was acquired by Middlesex County National Bank in 1947, and the building abandoned in 1965 for an existing building at 25 Nason Street. Middlesex acquired Assabet Savings Bank and moved into Assabet's building, adding "Middlesex Savings Bank" signage with an electronic clock and a semi-accurate temperature display.

The United Co-operative Society of Maynard started Maynard Consumers Credit Union in August 1948. It was at 64–66 Main Street and

Left: Middlesex Savings Bank sign on the building built for the Assabet Institution for Savings in 1929. The building itself has two dates gracing the front: 1929 for the building and 1904 for the bank's founding—Maynard's first bank.

Below: Maynard Trust Company was founded in 1913, constructed this building in 1926 and was bought out by Middlesex in 1947. For many years, the building was home to a branch office of the McWalter-Volunteer Insurance Agency, but as of 2020, it stands empty.

later at 68 Main Street, and it lasted until the end of the co-op in 1973. Bank-wise, there was then a quiet bank startup period until the 1970s, when a spate of branch banks opened: Community National Bank (1973, at 52 Main Street), Garden City Trust Company (1973), Concord Co-operative Bank (1978) and Digital Credit Union (1979). None is in Maynard now. DCU had branch offices in the mill and at 129 Parker Street. DCU survived the end of Digital Equipment Corporation, but the closest branch is in Acton. BayBank Middlesex moved into the building at 25 Nason Street in 1979 and then underwent a series of name changes, including BayBank, Fleet and lastly Bank of America (2004), which closed its doors in the fall of 2017. The most recent bank building to make an appearance in Maynard is at 47 Nason Street, opened as Garden City in 1973, later housing Concord Co-op and then Citizens Bank starting in 2001.

Traditionally, banks had impressive façades that often outlived the actual banks, leaving behind "ghost signs" on buildings that have been repurposed. "MAYNARD TRUST COMPANY" graces 75 Main Street. The building dates to 1926. The bank was acquired by Middlesex in 1947. Similarly, "ASSABET INSTITUTION FOR SAVINGS" is lettered atop Middlesex Bank at 17 Nason Street, the latter having acquired the former in 1988.

THE MILL AUCTIONED HOUSES IN 1934

Soon after having purchased the bankrupt Assabet Woolen Mill in May 1899, the American Woolen Company (AWC) expanded operations and decided to create housing to meet demands from workers. The company purchased farmland and pastureland on the east side of Parker Street in 1901 and over two years built 206 single-family homes and duplexes. This development became known as New Village as well as "Presidential Village," as the streets were named after presidents. Houses were rented to mill employees for three to six dollars per month. The Bancroft School (later renamed Calvin Coolidge School) was opened in September 1906, in part to accommodate children living in the new development.

In 1934, a smidge over thirty years later, the country was in the throes of the Great Depression, and the mill was operating at 20 percent capacity. AWC decided to auction housing in many towns, including in Maynard. On August 18 and 19, twelve vacant lots and 150 buildings in the Presidential Village development—single-family homes and duplexes—

150 DWELLINGS
101 Cottages, 49 Two Family Dwellings
12 Parcels Unimproved Land

At Public Auction to the Highest Bidder

FORMERLY PERTAINING TO THE

Assabet Mills

LOCATED IN THE TOWN OF

Maynard, Mass.

75% of the Purchase Price can Remain on Mortgage at 6%

ALL SALES ON THE PREMISES

Friday and Saturday, August 17 and 18, 1934

STARTING AT 10.00 A. M., DAYLIGHT SAVING TIME, EACH DAY

Local Office: Corner Waltham and Parker Streets. Open Daily

CALL UPON OUR REPRESENTATIVES FREELY FOR ANY INFORMATION YOU MAY DESIRE. THEY WILL BE PLEASED TO SHOW THE PROPERTIES AND EXPLAIN ALL DETAILS

Samuel T. Freeman & Co.
80 Federal Street, BOSTON, MASS.

AUCTIONEERS

Henry W. Cooke Co.
Hospital Trust Building
PROVIDENCE, R. I.

In the depths of the Great Depression, the American Woolen Company decided to auction all of the housing and non-mill commercial buildings it owned in Maynard. The auction was conducted by walking house to house. All of the properties found buyers, mostly town residents. *Courtesy of Maynard Historical Society.*

were auctioned, for a total of $183,740. All properties were sold. Terms were 10 percent at bid and 15 percent at closing; buyers were offered three-year mortgages on the remaining amount at 6 percent interest. The average for single-family homes was under $1,000. By way of comparison, a new Chevrolet car could be had for $450 to 700. The great majority of purchases were by Maynard residents.

This was actually the second AWC auction of 1934. June 23 of the same year saw the auction of seventy-four dwellings, many multi-family, plus four stores and three boardinghouses. Terms were the same as at the August auction. This sale included much of the company property on Main, Front and High Streets, plus the row house buildings on Railroad Street. The auction netted $90,000. Newspaper accounts of both auctions named the buyers, but not which properties they had bought.

A less well-known part of Maynard's history is that John F. Lovell, owner of Lovell Bus Lines, had accrued a notable amount of Maynard real estate

John Lovell, owner of the Lovell Bus Line, started bus service between Maynard and the South Acton train station in 1923, one month after the electric trolley ceased to provide the same connection. In time, Lovell bought the trolley car barn for his expanding bus service, which connected Maynard to surrounding and distant towns (as far as Revere Beach in the summer). Lovell died in 1945. His family continued the business to 1954 and then sold it to what became the MBTA. *Courtesy of Maynard Historical Society.*

and then auctioned twenty-four pieces of property to the highest bidders on December 2, 1939. The auction brochure included photos of each house, addresses, the selling prices and names of buyers. The terms were the same as at the 1934 auctions. The auctioneering firm, Samuel T. Freeman & Company, was also the same. From the brochure: "Accommodating from one to five families each. These properties have been excellently maintained, consistently occupied, and are advantageously located."

Lovell's letter to the auction house stated that he was eighty-two years old and had found that managing all this property in addition to the Lovell Bus Lines was too much of a burden. Most of what he owned comprised two- to five-family dwellings scattered about town. The total netted from the auction was about $55,000. Of note, what had been the Lorenzo Maynard mansion on Dartmouth Street, described as a five-family dwelling, went for $2,650. The building still exists as apartments, with the original stained-glass windows intact.

FUNERAL HOMES AND CEMETERIES

Henry Fowler, a signer of the 1871 petition to create the town of Maynard, was an undertaker. The term evolved from descriptions of men whose profession was to "under take" all arrangements for funerals. His son, Orrin S. Fowler, followed into the family business in 1887. Orrin and his wife, Nellie, were a power couple. He was on the founding boards of banks and held many town government offices. She was part of the DAR and was the first president of the American Legion Ladies Auxiliary. They were among the "honorables" on the very first electric trolley ride in 1901. Their son, Guyer Fowler (Harvard graduate, class of 1915, and World War I veteran who served in France), followed the family business until just before his death in 1956 at age sixty-three. Guyer was the one who moved the business to the Concord Street location in 1941. He sold it to John A. Kennedy, hence the name change to Fowler-Kennedy Funeral Home. This is the sole representative of the funeral business in Maynard today.

At one time, there were four. Herbert Martin started in 1927. Years later, his son-in-law, John Doran, joined the business, making it the Martin & Doran Funeral Home, and later moved to Acton. Sheehan and White Funeral Home operated on Bancroft Street into the 1970s. The W.A. Twombly Funeral Home had started out on Main Street near the Methodist church before relocating to 42 Summer Street and then closing in the 1950s.

What is now the Fowler-Kennedy Funeral Home business was started by Henry Fowler in 1871. In addition to being an undertaker, Fowler was a signer of the petition that led to the creation of Maynard and became one of Maynard's first selectmen. Fowler School is named after his son, Guyer W. Fowler.

Cemeteries

Prior to the founding of Maynard in 1871, most of the dead would have been buried in Sudbury or Stow. But with the start of church congregations in what was known as Assabet Village and the sense of becoming a community, people wanted to be buried closer to their families. Part of what is now Glenwood Cemetery was in use as a burial ground as far back as the 1850s. The first occupant after the cemetery was formally dedicated in 1871 was Thomas H. Brooks. St. Bridget's Cemetery also got off to an informal start, as a man named O'Donnell was interred in 1859, a decade before James Heffernan's official cemetery burial. The present-day stone wall and entrances were added in 1900. Both cemeteries are still active.

Formally, Glenwood started with eight acres purchased from the Maynard family. The family kept one corner for the Maynard crypt, completed in 1881. In time, more land was purchased from Lorenzo Maynard and then eleven acres from the Taylor family in 1928. That year saw the replacement

This 1903 photo shows the original iron gate entrance to Glenwood Cemetery, replaced in 1928. In the background is a gazebo that was destroyed by the 1938 hurricane, as were many of the spruce trees (replaced by sugar maple). *Courtesy of Maynard Historical Society.*

of the original iron gateway with the present-day granite archway entrance that bears a sign: "This Gateway presented to the Town of Maynard by William F. Litchfield 1928." Litchfield was a dealer in coal and firewood, using the slogan "From mine to cellar." His office and coal yard were on Main Street, just west of the Assabet River. He and his wife, Amy (a descendent of the Smith family), lived in the large white house the Smith family had owned at 38 Great Road, corner of Summer Hill and Great Road. To this day, there is a very large piece of anthracite coal set in the yard between the barn and the road.

A roadside crypt was constructed in 1888, with that date set over the door and no family name. This was designed to temporarily host the deceased in winter, when the ground was too frozen to dig a grave. Over 2013–15, the Maynard Historical Commission, though use of Community Preservation Act and Perpetual Care funds, saw to replacement of the iron fence bordering Glenwood Cemetery. The fence it replaced had been erected in the 1930s as part of the Depression-era Works Progress Administration of the New Deal; the new fence is a historically accurate replica of its predecessor. The hurricane of 1938 blew down most of the original spruce trees and damaged the gazebo that had graced the cemetery just inside the entrance. Replacement plantings were mostly sugar maples. Of note, Glenwood Cemetery is the only property in town that is in the National Register of Historic Places.

Counting the Dead

All this history begs the question: How many people are buried in Maynard? The estimate, roughly 11,700, comes from a combination of asking and counting and guessing. The records for St. Bridget's Cemetery are fairly good. The church's count is about 5,000. Town records for Glenwood Cemetery are incomplete. Rumor has it that some were used in the cemetery shed's potbellied stove as fire starters. Peg Brown, one of Maynard's self-appointed amateur historians, took up the project of counting the dead. Her unofficial database—compiled from official records and headstone readings in 2013—listed 6,766 names, along with section and lot numbers, plus the year of death for the great majority. The addition of those two counts is in fairly close accord with a tallying of deaths reported in the town's annual reports. This may be an undercount, as when towns bring in ground-penetrating radar they often tentatively identify unrecorded graves.

DEPRESSION-ERA PUBLIC WORKS PROJECTS

During the depths of the multi-year Great Depression, the federal government's role in America grew more than in any era before. During this time between 1932 and 1940, there were numerous examples of growth of the government. About thirty-two new government agencies were created during the eight-year period. While many of the agencies formed have been abolished or replaced by another, some agencies still stand today. Historian William Leuchtenburg wrote, "The six years from 1933 through 1938 marked a greater upheaval in American institutions than in any similar period in our history."

The town's annual reports provide a description of how the worsening depression overwhelmed local efforts and then how federal programs provided support. From the 1931 Report of the Public Welfare Board: "Nineteen Hundred Thirty-one has been a sad year for most of the people of Maynard....We sincerely hope the worst has passed and that we will never see as poor a year again." Town programs included Mothers Aid Cases, Old Age Assistance and Temporary Aid. There was more of the same the next year, with able-bodied men on aid doing street and sidewalk work. The wool and gunpowder mills loaned land to be used for municipal gardens, providing fresh vegetables, potatoes and beans. A canning operation was started.

The federal agencies most active in Maynard were the Emergency Relief Administration (ERA, 1932), which became the Federal Emergency Relief Administration (FERA, 1993), to be replaced by the Works Progress Administration (WPA, 1935). Also active locally was the Civil Works Administration (CWA 1933). The CWA put able-bodied men and women on payroll. The ERA paid one-third costs of people on welfare, while also providing free food, coal and firewood for people in need.

By 1934, some 100 to 175 residents of Maynard were on ERA or CWA payrolls. Labor went to sidewalks, storm drains and improvements at Crowe Park. The municipal gardens program continued. This was also the year that the woolen mill, operating at only 20 percent capacity, auctioned off 236 pieces of property—mostly single-family homes but also business buildings and rooming houses. The following year's support continued to include federal surplus food and clothing. The Works Progress Administration implemented the Sewing Project, which employed thirty women. The gardens canning project put up thirty thousand cans of vegetables, helping support Maynard and neighboring towns.

Construction of the stone-walled fieldhouse at Alumni Field was started by the FERA in 1933–35 and completed by the WPA in 1938. *Courtesy of Maynard Historical Society.*

The year 1936 saw the startup of the Social Security Act, which helped provide for the elderly. The Sewing Project, operating out of Roosevelt School, made dresses, shirts, pajamas, bedsheets and more. More of the same took place in 1937, but toward the end of 1938, there began a trend of people finding private employment. WPA hires diminished by half. Some of the work in this and following years included first clearing land and then planting hundreds of trees to replace all the damage wrought by the 1938 hurricane. The town's annual report for 1941 mentioned that the woolen mill was operating at full capacity, filling military orders for blankets and wool cloth for coats. The Sewing Project was ended. The number of general relief cases was the lowest it had been since 1929.

The website The Living New Deal lists Depression-era projects by town. Many were routine construction or maintenance, but a few were interesting additions to Maynard's ambiance (so many now lost, sadly). Routine tasks included painting, windows repair and more at schools, the poor farm and fire house, as well as work on streets, sidewalks, water mains and storm sewers. Additionally, the Mill Street bridge was rebuilt in 1937. Glenwood Cemetery gained an iron fence, the new section was created and the corner of Routes 27 and 117 was converted from a swamp to an ice skating pond, with an island in the middle and a pond in the middle of the island. This has since reverted to swamp/bog. Crowe Park was upgraded in 1935. A fieldstone bandstand was constructed in Crowe Park in 1939; by the 1990s, it was in disrepair and was torn down. Fieldstone construction also graced the gates and fieldhouse at Alumni Field (still standing) and a "comfort station" (public restroom) behind Memorial Park, removed to create a parking lot.

THE GREAT LAND EVICTION OF WORLD WAR II

A bit more than one-fifth of Maynard was seized by the federal government via eminent domain in the spring of 1942. Residents were given as little as ten days to vacate their houses and farms. The land—3,100 acres in Maynard, Sudbury, Hudson and Stow (800 in Maynard)—was taken to create a munitions storage and transfer site. Years after the war, the land was turned over to the "Natick Army Labs" for product field testing and then to the army's Fort Devens for training exercises. All this became an Environmental

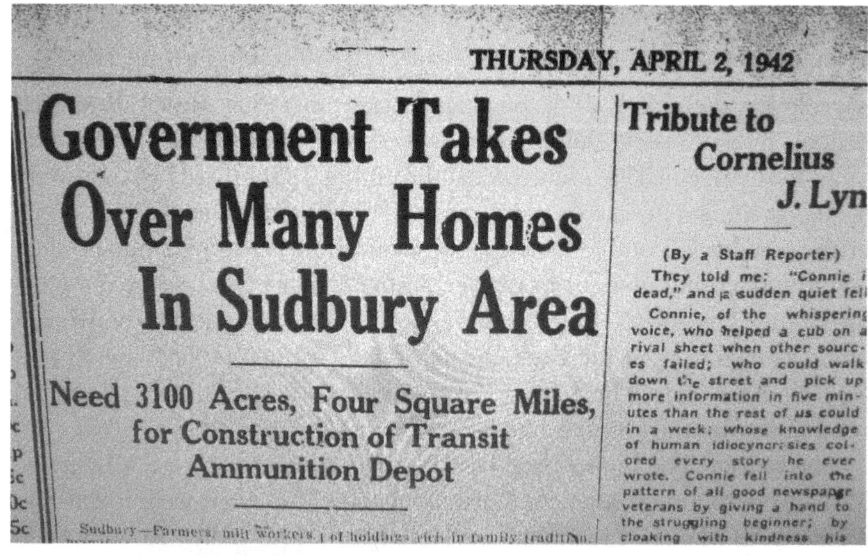

THURSDAY, APRIL 2, 1942

Government Takes Over Many Homes In Sudbury Area

Need 3100 Acres, Four Square Miles, for Construction of Transit Ammunition Depot

Sudbury—Farmers, mill workers, of holdings rich in family tradition

Tribute to Cornelius J. Lyn

(By a Staff Reporter)

They told me: "Connie i dead," and a sudden quiet fel Connie, of the whispering voice, who helped a cub on a rival sheet when other sources failed; who could walk down the street and pick up more information in five minutes than the rest of us could in a week; whose knowledge of human idiosyncrasies colored every story he ever wrote. Connie fell into the pattern of all good newspaper veterans by giving a hand to the struggling beginner; by cloaking with kindness his

A *Boston Globe* headline from 1942: "Government Takes Over Many Homes in Sudbury Area." *Courtesy of Stow Historical Society.*

Protection Agency "Superfund" cleanup site before its transformation into a national wildlife refuge.

Working backward in time, the visitor center at Assabet River National Wildlife Refuge opened in October 2010, which was five years after the 2,230-acre refuge was opened to the public. There was a five-year preparation period before that, starting when the site was turned over to U.S. Fish & Wildlife Service in 2000. The refuge's specific objectives include the conservation and management of migratory bird species; the restoration of wetland, grassland and forest habitats; and natural resource related education. Public use of the refuge includes wildlife observation, photography, environmental education, hunting and fishing.

Prior to the release of land from military control, it was most recently the Fort Devens–Sudbury Training Annex (1982–2000); the United States Army Natick Soldier Research, Development and Engineering Center before that (1958–82); and the Maynard Ordnance Supply Depot and then the Maynard Ordnance Test Station before that (1942–58). Fort Devens was involved in 1990 when the area was categorized as a "Superfund" cleanup site because of contamination with volatile organic compounds, arsenic, pesticides and other chemicals. Arsenic compounds had been used as herbicides to keep the railroad tracks clear of weeds during the time of munitions storage. Extensive EPA-supervised army cleanup efforts included removing more than fifteen thousand cubic yards of contaminated soil, removing hundreds of buried fifty-five-gallon metal containers filled with chemical waste, covering a two-acre landfill with a water-impermeable cap and monitoring groundwater. Afterward, as the land and waterways were still too contaminated to allow residential or commercial development, a decision was made to create a wildlife refuge.

Natick Army Labs contributed to the contamination problem during its tenure. Its function is the research and development of food, clothing (including flame-retardant clothing tests), shelters, airdrop systems and other service member support items for the U.S. military. Laboratory waste was buried in a landfill pit.

The initial taking of land in 1942 had been for the creation of a munitions transfer site. Railroad tracks were laid from the west, leading to the doors of fifty widely spaced bunkers. Each of the bunkers, officially referred to as "igloos," has an interior dimension of eighty-one by twenty-six by twelve feet. Sides and roofs were mounded with dirt for extra protection and disguise. Convoys of trucks would convey munitions to the harbor for ships heading to Europe. Today, from all but the door end, these bunkers

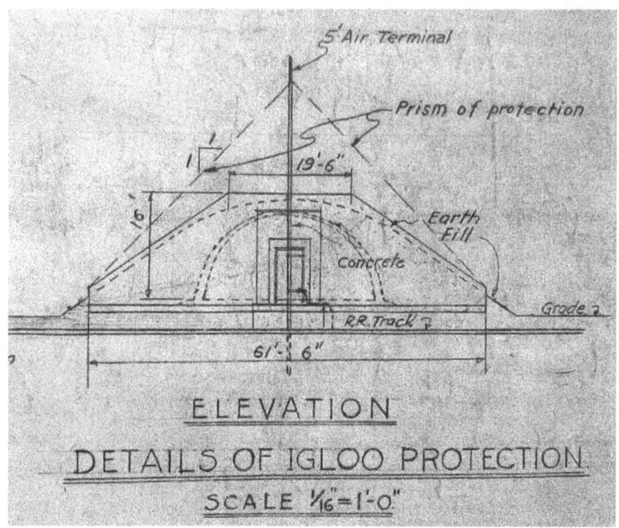

Railroad tracks crossed the face of each bunker. The "Air Terminal" in the blueprint was a lightning rod, tall enough to provide a "prism of protection" for the entire structure. There are no mentions of any explosions occurring during the years this operated as a munition depot.

resemble small hills, complete with a forest of trees growing on top. After the war, transfer activity stopped, but the army chose to use the site for munitions testing rather than return land to former owners, as they had been verbally promised.

As to those owners, it was March 1942 when surveyors showed up and started the process of expropriating land held by more than one hundred landowners, mostly farmland, with some of the homesteads dating back to the early 1700s. A *Boston Globe* reporter came out and interviewed several of the families. Statements such as "It's the least we can do" and "It's a small part to play in helping to win the war" were attributed to displaced homeowners. The reality, gleaned from postwar interviews with some of the same families, was that they were in shock; they had been told that they had to get off their land without even knowing how much they might get paid. Their abandoned houses and barns were either immediately demolished or left to decay, torn down later.

When our government takes land through eminent domain, "it has a constitutional responsibility to justly compensate the property owner for the fair market value of the property." There were claims that the evicted people received ten cents on the dollar for property value. There is no documentation for this. It's true that people were forced to hurriedly sell or auction furniture, farm equipment and farm animals, much at below their true worth, but payments for land may have been closer to market value. One example cited as documenting the unfairness was the Suikko family being paid $5,700 for the forty-six-acre farm they had purchased twenty-three years earlier for $6,500. However, this time interval was one of deflation rather than inflation, so the land may have truly been valued less than when it had been purchased. Payment, even if fair or close to fair, did not mitigate the pain of being forced off one's land on short notice and without recourse nor any subsequent opportunity to return after the war.

POLICE AND FIRE DEPARTMENTS

Police

At the very first town meeting on April 27, 1871, the need for law enforcement was seen as essential. Three constables were elected. Responsibilities included keeping the peace, distributing town warrants and, for an additional ten dollars per year, serving as school truant officers. The following month, the town approved construction of a brick lockup, fourteen feet square, consisting of two cells. The location was behind No. 2 Railroad Street. Twenty years later, the town voted to build a new lockup, also of brick, behind the Nason Street fire station. It was in use until 1934; it was demolished in 1984 to make way for the Paper Store building at 36 Nason Street.

As late as 1900, the entire annual budget for the police department was $500 per year, but with the growth after the American Woolen Company bought and enlarged the mill, a larger police force became necessary. In 1930, crosswalks and yellow lines were painted in various places for the first time for traffic safety, indicating increased automobile traffic. A few years later, police headquarters, including a lockup, was moved to the building on the west side of town hall. The department got its first police car in 1938, added a two-way radio in 1946 and became responsible for managing the newly installed parking meters in 1951. Recent years have the meters bringing in about $40,000 and parking tickets $20,000.

On October 4, 1955, the department moved into the new combination police and fire station at the corner of Summer and Main Streets, to reside there for fifty-four years. After several years of planning and failed attempts to get voter approval, a new station got a yes vote at town meeting in 2007. The site was the building west of town hall, recently vacated by the Maynard Public Library, which had moved in 2006 into what had been Roosevelt School. The board of selectmen attended the groundbreaking ceremony on April 22, 2008, and the ribbon-cutting ceremony one year later.

The second Maynard jailhouse (seen here) was operative from 1891 to 1934 but not demolished until 1984. (This begs the question of what it was being used for in the interim.) The location was behind Maynard's first fire station (1891–1955) at 36 Nason Street. *Courtesy of Maynard Historical Society.*

The police department uniform patch has its own history. From 1965 to 1982, it featured an eagle clutching arrows and an olive branch, as well as a shield, all loosely borrowed from the Great Seal of the United States. In 1982, the clock tower replaced the stripes on the shield. Ten years later, the shield contained the present-day Maynard seal, with a smaller eagle clutching the U.S. and Massachusetts flags. Lastly, in 2007, the eagle vanished, leaving space for the town seal centered on a blue background, with the words MAYNARD (above) POLICE (below). The trim on the clock tower image is shown as bright red.

Today, the Maynard Police Department headquarters is adjacent to town hall. Staffing includes twenty-one officers (two women) and seven civilians, mostly dispatchers. Fire and police communications (dispatch) were combined into one communications center in 2015. Maynard has 2.0 officers per 1,000 people. That is below the national average of 2.4 per 1,000. The completion of the Assabet River Rail Trail catalyzed a decision to purchase two electric-powered bicycles.

According to city-data.com, the 2018 crime index in Maynard was smaller than the U.S. average but higher than in surrounding towns. "Crime index"

The plaque on wall at Maynard's police department matches the uniform badge.

is a City Data score that combines crimes against people and crimes against property. The great majority of reported crimes are thefts of property. There have been no murders in the past twenty-five years. Week after week, the police report in the *Beacon Villager* is mostly loose/lost animals, vehicle accidents, family disputes and arrests for impaired driving.

The town has not always been so benign. From 1900 to 1940, there was a murder almost every other year! Circumstances were the usual: robbery, revenge, jealousy and more. Lorenzo Barnes murdered Acton Street resident John Dean in 1896 after robbing him of seventy dollars; Barnes was the last criminal in Massachusetts to be executed by hanging. In 1919, Luigi Graceffa was found floating in Charles River with knife wounds. He had testified as a witness in a murder case in Waltham, and this was thought to be a revenge killing. Referred to in the *Boston Globe* as the "Mill Pond Murder," Lila Taryma, mother of four, disappeared the Saturday evening before Easter Sunday 1953. Her body was found weeks later in the millpond, lashed to a heavy radiator. Cause of death was head injuries. Her husband, Anthony Taryma, was initially charged with her murder. They had been seen arguing at a bar that evening, but he left and she remained. Anthony was not brought to trial due to insufficient evidence.

Police Chiefs

From 1902 to 1925, the chairman of the board of selectmen acted as chief of police. After that came John Connors (1925–36), Henry F. Piecewicz (1937–54), Michael T. Zapareski (1955–68), Albert J. Crowley (1968–80), Arner S. Tibbetts (1980–86 as interim chief, 1986–94), Edward M. Lawton (1994–99), James F. Corcoran (1999–2012), Mark Dubois (2012–19) and Michael A. Noble (2019–present).

Fire

The Town of Maynard appointed three fire wardens at its very first town meeting in 1871; it did not get around to organizing a fire department until 1890. One factor for Maynard's municipal involvement in firefighting not being a high priority was, basically, that there was not much a fire department could do. Well into the 1800s, "Getting the wet stuff on the red stuff" meant men running to the fire with buckets and forming a bucket line from the nearest well. Water would either be thrown directly at the fire or poured into a tank on a fire wagon, after which hand-powered pumps provided water pressure. Later innovations included leather hoses and hook and ladder wagons.

In Maynard, a town reservoir was constructed in 1888 atop Summer Hill. A water delivery system, including fifty-seven fire hydrants, was completed in 1889. Maynard's first fire station was constructed at 36 Nason Street in 1891. The initial major pieces of equipment were a hose wagon and a ladder wagon. Volunteers committed to show up as quickly as possible when the alarm whistle sounded. The first full-time employee was hired in 1903. The first gas-powered fire truck was purchased in 1914.

The original fire house served until 1955, when the current building on Summer Street was completed, with five thousand square feet dedicated to fire station operations. Construction costs were less than what one ladder truck costs now. Town documents described the fire department as having two firemen on duty at all times (with the off-duty men on call) and two equipment vehicles (fire truck and ladder truck), servicing 150 to 200 incidents per year. Emergency medical services/ambulance duties were added in 1976.

On-duty staff has increased, as have the number of vehicles. Medical calls responses number more than 1,000 per year, with total calls at more than 1,500—out of the same space. As of 2020, staffing was twenty-one firefighters and six "call" firefighters. Equipment is an ambulance, one aerial ladder truck, two trucks, a "brush" truck and a command car. The 2018 budget was a tad over $2 million. A new fire station is long overdue. The intent is to build a new station on Sudbury Street, near St. Bridget's Church.

Over decades, more than a dozen public buildings had serious fires. At the crossing of Summer and Nason Streets, there have been three fires, at Riverside Cooperative, Fraternal Order of Eagles and Maynard Hotel. Booth's Bowling Alley burned in 1906. Suspicions at the time were that a pet monkey, which had the run of the place at night and knew how to strike

Firemen and the driver looking very spiffy in this 1925 photo. *Courtesy of Maynard Historical Society.*

The morning after the Nason Street school fire of September 20, 1916, all that was left standing were the foundation and the two chimneys. The Roosevelt School was built on the foundation. The stonework arch is now the entrance to the library. *Courtesy of Maynard Historical Society.*

matches, was responsible for the fire (the monkey suffered burns but survived). The trolley car house and cars went up in flames in 1921. Upstream of the dam, the Bent Ice House burned in 1919. A replacement was built on the same foundation. That one burned 1950.

In the modern era, the two-story building on Main Street that housed Salsalito's Restaurant and T.C. Lando's Sub & Pizzeria was consumed by flames in 1998; NAPA Auto Parts was damaged in 2001, and Gruber Bros. Furniture suffered a smoky fire a decade before ending the business, an echo of a much larger fire in that building in 1934.

To paraphrase Robert Frost, someone there is that doesn't love a school—often a student. This is not to hint that school fires do not happen by accident. But history records five school fires: Nason Street School in 1879, Nason Street School 1916, Woodrow Wilson School 1952, Emerson-Fowler School in 1977 and Maynard High School in 1992. There is no record of any church fires.

Fire Horns and Hydrants

For more than a century, the fire department was responsible for conducting a daily 12:10 p.m. fire alarm test. In older days, this was a battery-powered striker hitting the school bell, then a blast of the fire department's steam whistle (located at the mill), then a diaphone horn at the fire station on Nason Street and then compressed air horns from the roof of the Summer Street fire house. The fire horn no longer sounds. The decision was made by the fire department in 2011. The equipment was in poor repair and heading toward obsolescence; if needed, off-duty staff are notified via cellphone. This begs the question: Can a sound be historic? Should Maynard's 12:10 horn be restored as a tradition when the horn no longer serves a practical purpose?

Fire hydrants, on the other hand, are eminently practical. Maynard in the late 1880s had a population of 2,500 and no central water system. Pumps and pipes were installed to bring water three miles north from White Pond, Sudbury. The initial system had 7,500 feet of iron pipe and fifty-seven fire hydrants. Subsequent Town of Maynard annual reports mention more pipe and hydrants being added as the town grew. Settled Maynard was very compact at the time; today it's more spread out population is on the order of 10,000 people, serviced by a roughly estimated four hundred to five hundred fire hydrants.

Most of the fire hydrants in Maynard read "Mueller," "Albertville" and either "ALA" or "AL" (for Alabama), plus a year for when the hydrant was made. Pre-1975 Muellers are identified as being made in "Chatta Tenn" (for Chattanooga, Tennessee). Mueller Company was started in 1857 and got into the hydrant business in 1933. Older hydrants are painted white with a colored top; newer hydrants are all red. The apparent winner for oldest hydrant is located on an unpaved portion of White Avenue. Buried under uncounted layers of white paint, the hydrant has an emblem of a "C" entwined with a "V," which stands for Chapman Valve. A raised circle surrounds the emblem with the faintly legible words "Chapman Valve" on the top and "Boston" on the bottom. Outside this ring is a stylized snowflake design. All this detail dates the hydrant's manufacture to 1890–1900. However, Winter Avenue itself and neighboring streets were created in 1921. The possibility remains that this is one of Maynard's first hydrants, installed at the same time as the beginnings of the town's water system, later relocated to Winter Avenue.

The Maynard Fire Department is in the slow process of deactivating and removing some seventy-plus "Gamewell" fire alarm boxes, the end of a system that saw its first installation in 1892.

NEWSPAPERS

Maynard has been served by several newspapers over the years. Starting at the present and working backward, we have the *Beacon-Villager* for Maynard and Stow. It's a weekly. It shows up Thursdays, as home delivery and in stores. Holly Camaro has been the editor and major reporter since August 2013. Of late, it runs as sixteen pages, but in the past it has been twenty-four or even thirty-two pages. The *B-V* is owned by Gannett Company, the largest newspaper publisher in the United States. The *B-V* owner had gone by the name Gatehouse Media until November 2019, when Gatehouse acquired Gannett and then took the Gannett name. In Massachusetts, Gatehouse had already owned *MetroWest Daily News* and more than one hundred town weekly papers, publishing in print and at town-by-town websites.

The *Beacon*, started in Acton, was the forerunner of the *Beacon-Villager*. It launched in 1945. In the summer of 1953, the Beacon Publishing Company was the first business to move into Maynard's mill after the conversion from woolen goods factory to rentable office and industry space. As the

VOLUNTEER OF THE WEEK: SKYLAN ZAYAS

'THE HUNT' WAS WORTH THE WAIT

Beacon-Villager

Serving Maynard and Stow

Thursday, March 19, 2020 | Maynard.WickedLocal.com • Stow.WickedLocal.com | facebook.com/beaconvillager/ | Vol. 61, No. 12 | $2

ONLINE

CORONAVIRUS UPDATES ON OUR WEBSITE

Fire damages Maynard home

No one home at time of blaze

By Robert Fucci

A four-alarm fire on Sunday, March 15, left significant smoke and fire damage to the home that housed two residents.

According to Maynard Fire Chief Anthony Stowers, at approximately 2:20 p.m., the Maynard Fire Department was dispatched to 14 Walcott St. for a possible structure fire. Upon arrival, crews discovered heavy smoke and fire coming from the home and quickly went to a second alarm.

A third alarm was struck at 2:35 p.m. and ultimately went to a fourth alarm to rotate crews.

There was heavy fire on two floors. The fire was deemed under control just after 4 p.m.

Neither of the two occupants were at home at the time of the fire. No firefighters were injured.

Crews from Stow, Sudbury, Lincoln, Acton, Weston, Marlborough, Hudson, Wayland, Carlisle, Bedford, Boxborough, Pro-ALS, the Mass Department of Fire Services Rehabilitation Unit, Fire District 14 Communications Team, and the Massachusetts Fire District 14 Chiefs Assistance Team, as well as the Maynard Police Department.

See FIRE, A5

A Maynard firefighter looks at flames shooting from the roof during the four-alarm fire at 14 Walcott St. in Maynard, March 15.

Maynard has had weekly newspaper coverage since 1888: *Maynard Enterprise* (1888–1970), the *Maynard News* (1899–1943) and the *Beacon-Villager* (1945–present).

Beacon and later the *Assabet Valley Beacon*, it served several towns. In time, this evolved to papers for each town, including Acton's *Beacon*, the *Concord Free Press* and the *Sudbury Citizen*.

Rolling the years back, the *Maynard News*, published in Hudson, serviced the towns of Maynard, Hudson, South Acton, Stow and Concord Junction (West Concord). It started in 1899 and ceased publication in 1943. What is surprising is how little actual "news" was in the paper. Week after week, the pages were filled with announcement-type items, such as a wrestling match at the Finnish Hall, a lecture on the "White Slave Trade," engagement announcements and school concerts. Apparently, the main function of the newspapers of a century ago appears to have been akin to what we now think of social media—personal items people wanted to share with the community. Most of the old issues exist as bound folios at the Maynard Historical Society (MHS) and on microfilm at the Maynard Public Library.

The *Enterprise Weekly*, later renamed to *Maynard Enterprise*, predated the *Maynard News* by eleven years, was headquartered in Marlborough and covered surrounding towns. Individual copies were $0.03 and a year's subscription $1.00. Advertisements were interesting. A century ago, Distasio's Market offered beef at $0.15 to $0.25 per pound. Lerer's Clothing Store had men's shoes for $2.00 and suits for $10.00 to $20.00. Another ad offered an oak dining room table with six chairs for only $25.00. Ford Motor Company offered car models starting at $700.00. To put all this into perspective, factory pay was less than $2.00 per day. The *Enterprise* ceased publication in 1970.

The oldest record of newspaper content about Maynard is from an unidentified paper (possibly the *Concord Freeman*, 1875–85). What exists is a handful of pages in the MHS collection dated 1879. Among the typical coverage of bridge club outings and people taken ill was a mention that the Maynard family was vacationing in New Hampshire and hoped to visit Mount Washington.

Chapter 6
DOWNTOWN

Main, Summer and Nason Streets form a triangle that can be considered the core of Maynard's downtown. Summer is ancient, while the other two date to 1849. Flanking these streets were churches, meeting halls, hotels, schools, movie theaters, co-operatives and other stores, boardinghouses and apartment buildings, restaurants, bars, pool halls, bowling alleys and buildings of several of the town's fraternal societies. The trolley brought people from neighboring towns to shop in Maynard. The train connected Maynard to Boston. Hundreds came to free band concerts performed at the bandstand at the corner of Walnut and Main. Time (and fire) demolished many of the old buildings, but the compactness of downtown Maynard and the new businesses there contribute to making it vibrantly walkable.

A CHANGE OF CHURCHES

The closing of churches and synagogues is not unique to Maynard. Across the United States, what are referred to as the mainline Protestant churches have been undergoing a prolonged decline in attendance, membership and number of parishes since the 1960s. Estimates are that membership has dropped by half. By contrast, membership in Catholic and Evangelical churches has been increasing, albeit not as fast as the population increase as a whole. An additional problem for Maynard was that construction of the places of worship predated the commonality of car ownership and thus lacked the parking lots essential for a more widely distributed congregation.

From Oldest to Newest Based on When Services Started

- Union Congregational Church, 1852–2017 (church built in 1853)
- St. Bridget's Roman Catholic Church, 1866–present (first church in 1871, current church in 1884)
- United Methodist Church of Maynard, 1867–2014 (church built in 1895)
- St. George's Episcopal Church, 1895–2006 (church built in 1895)
- St. John's Evangelical Lutheran Church, 1902–67 (church built in 1907)
- Mission Evangelical Congregational Church, 1906–2020 (church built in 1913)
- St. Casimir Catholic Church, 1912–97 (church bought the building in 1928; had been trolley power station 1901–23)
- Holy Annunciation Orthodox Church, 1915–present (church built in 1917)
- Congregation Rodoff Shalom, 1921–80 (house converted to synagogue in 1921)
- Kingdom Hall of Jehovah's Witnesses, 1960–present (hall built in 1967)
- Church of the Nazarene, 1968–present (in what had been St. John's, 1968–95)
- St. Stephen's Knanaya Church, 1990–present (building had been Finnish Temperance Society "Alku" in 1910–67, VFW Post No. 1812, 1967–88; purchased by St. Stephen's in 1992)
- St. Mary's Indian Orthodox Church, 1991–present (purchased St. Casimir building in 2003)
- First Bible Baptist Church, ????–present

The Union Congregational Church (1852–2017) was Maynard's first parish, established as an Evangelical Union Society in 1850, when eight local residents decided to form a Sunday school. This predated the creation of the town of Maynard by twenty-one years. Amory Maynard became the Sunday school's first superintendent. The next step was to engage a

Congregational Church in a snowy haze. The church closed in 2017. The building was repurposed as a rentable meeting place: The Sanctuary.

preacher for Sunday services. Both school and services took place in the newly constructed train station. Prior to this, people walked or traveled by wagon the three miles to Stow's Evangelical Church.

Within a few years, these residents of Assabet Village incorporated as a church and selected a committee to find a site to build a house of worship. What came to pass is that Amory and his business partner, William Knight, donated land on Main Street, and the building was constructed, financed by members. Buying in got these families reserved pews, as was a common practice of that era. The cost of construction and furnishings came to $3,876. The original name was the American Congregational Church.

Here's a sampling of important dates: The steeple acquired a bell in 1855. The church acquired its first organ in 1959. The church was enlarged in 1866. In the early 1890s, Deacon Lorenzo Maynard (son of Amory Maynard) contributed funds for stained-glass windows in the church. Four of the windows bear the names of his daughters—Frances, Mary, Victoria and Hattie—who predeceased him. He also donated toward the addition of the building on the west side, to house a chapel and classrooms, including a glorious stained-glass portrait of Jesus holding a lamb, over the words "I Am the Good Shepherd." The building had no steeple from 1909 to 1920, the original having been blown off the building in a storm. The church was officially renamed the Union Congregational Church in 1927. The bell was replaced by chimes in the mid-1940s.

The church ceased services in 2017. In September of that year, it was purchased by Maynard resident William Doyle and reopened in 2019 as The Sanctuary, a performance space. The interior has been remodeled for space suitable for events, concerts, wedding receptions and more.

St. Bridget's Roman Catholic Church had its beginnings with priests from the Saxonville (Framingham) Parish periodically visiting Assabet Village to hold Mass services in people's homes. By 1857, the number of Catholic families in Assabet were so many that monthly Mass was held in Union Hall. The year 1866 saw the dedication of a Catholic church, located on Main Street, just east of the location of the present-day town hall. In 1871, this officially became St. Bridget's Parish. This status was short-lived; a severe, international economic depression caused the local congregation to be downgraded to a mission of St. Bernard's, Concord. Despite this status, the Catholic population—primarily immigrants from Ireland—continued to increase. In 1881, the site of the present-day church was purchased from Amory Maynard. The cornerstone was laid in 1881, the completed building

St. Bridget's as it appeared in 1900, with Reverend John A. Crowe as pastor. Note the taller steeple than at present—the change was made after damage by the 1938 hurricane—and a shed in back for people who arrived by horse and carriage. *Courtesy of Maynard Historical Society.*

was dedicated in 1884 and the reestablishment of St. Bridget's as its own parish took place in 1894. Reverend John A. Crowe, who served as pastor from 1894 to 1905, oversaw the purchase of a nearby house to serve as a rectory. He also was responsible for the purchase and installation of a Hook and Hastings organ, which serves to this day.

A hurricane in 1938 severely damaged the building. A replacement steeple, though shorter, was built, and the three wooden flights of stairs across the front were replaced with brick. The windows over the main altar, blown out by the storm, were also replaced.

In 1869, St. Bridget's Parish obtained land along Great Road (Route 117), east of Maynard's Glenwood Cemetery, to create St. Bridget's Cemetery. The first official burial was of James Heffernan, a Civil War veteran, buried on April 12, 1870. (A few headstones predate 1869; they either predate the cemetery proper or had been set on private land elsewhere and then relocated.) Over time, more land was added. The stone wall and entrance arch were added in 1900. A rough estimate is that five thousand people are interred there.

There is often a gestation period between first services and steeple—for the United Methodist Church, this was almost 30 years. Services began in 1867 but were held in various meeting halls until the congregation completed the existing building in 1895. May 11, 2014, saw the last Sunday services at UMC, ending 119 years in the building and 147 years as a congregation. Members began joining other churches. The local Alcoholics Anonymous groups, which had used the church for its meetings, relocated within town.

At St. George's Episcopal Church, Episcopal services began in 1894. The cornerstone of the church was placed on August 10, 1895; the church was consecrated as the Parish of St. George in 1897. The church had an active men's group, the Order of Sir Galahad; a women's group, the Guild of St. Hilda; and a youth summer camp program at Fort Pond. Membership declined after the Church of the Good Shepherd opened in Acton in 1962. After the Maynard church closed, the parking lot and rectory were sold separately. The church was remodeled to a duplex condominium, but the steeple remains, topped by a cross.

St. John's Evangelical Lutheran Church was incorporated as the Finnish Evangelical Lutheran Church in 1902. August 1894 had seen an outdoor service in Finnish on the banks of the millpond, an event proposed by a traveling Bible salesman. The event served as a catalyst to start a Lutheran church. In 1902, the nascent congregation bought land on Glendale Street. Construction started in 1907; the church was dedicated on June 6, 1908. The congregation stayed active, although over years the members and their children and grandchildren assimilated (services switched from Finnish to English). The name change to St. John's occurred in 1945. In 1967, the congregation decided to construct a new church in north Sudbury (with its own parking lot). The Church of the Nazarene took up residence for a while and then moved out around 1995. The building was deconsecrated and became a private residence.

The Mission Evangelical Congregational Church was organized in 1906 as the Finnish Evangelical Congregational Church. During the early years, services were held at the Union Congregational Church. The congregation's own church, on Walnut Street, was constructed and dedicated in 1913. The name change took place in 1967 because by then most of the congregation spoke English and services were held in English. The congregation decided to sell the church in 2019. As of 2020, the church building is for sale.

By 1910, more than six hundred immigrants from Poland were living in Maynard. They wanted to hear sermons and other aspects of church service in their own language. A parish for the ST. CASIMIR ROMAN CATHOLIC CHURCH—with services in Polish—was established in 1912, meeting at St. Bridget's. Fourteen years passed before the congregation bought the powerhouse building of the defunct Concord, Maynard and Hudson Railway (electric trolley), and two more years passed before the converted building was blessed as their own church.

In time, death of first-generation immigrants, assimilation of their descendants and dearth of new immigrants placed a toll on all of Greater Boston's Polish parishes. In 1995, Cardinal Bernard Law announced that ten of fourteen parishes would stop celebrating Mass in Polish. Four years later, the *Beacon-Villager* ran an article about the pending closure of St. Casimir. A locally circulated petition could not reverse the decision. The parish was merged back into St. Bridget Parish, although the St. Casimir building remained a consecrated space, used by the Polish community for baptisms, weddings and funerals. In 2003, the building was sold to St. Mary's Indian Orthodox Church of Boston.

The start of the HOLY ANNUNCIATION ORTHODOX CHURCH presence in Maynard began as many congregations do, with a visiting priest conducting a service in a private home. The church, on Prospect Street, topped with the blue domes of Russian rural church architecture, became a reality in 1917 (the cornerstone dated to 1916). A bell was acquired in 1920 and a chandelier added in 1923. Its beginnings were as a parish of the Russian Orthodox Church in America, services in Old Church Slavonic. Many of the congregants were workers at the woolen mill—the three-barred Cross of the ROC can be seen on tombstones at Glenwood Cemetery. Over decades, Russian and then English were incorporated into services. In 1970, the Russian Orthodox Church in America received its autocephaly (right to self-government) from the Mother Church in Russia, becoming the "Orthodox Church in America." Membership is not limited to particular ethnic groups or nationalities. While a Russian immigrant presence in Maynard has long diminished, the church serves people of Orthodox faith from Maynard and the surrounding communities.

Prior to the start of CONGREGATION RODOFF SHALOM, both the Ednas Israel Society and the Maynard Hebrew Society (MHS) arranged to have rabbis from other towns hold services in rented halls. Then, in 1921, MHS bought a house on Nason Street and had it moved to Acton Street, to serve as Rodoff Shalom Synagogue (the building still stands as a private residence). In the 1960s, a growing Jewish community in Acton was attending services in Maynard, but in time it grew too large. The Acton group incorporated as Congregation Beth Elohim and then in 1980 consecrated a synagogue. Rodoff Shalom closed. The Torah was removed from the Ark and, with a police escort, walked north on Route 27 to Beth Elohim, with congregants holding a chuppah over the Torah and others blowing shofars.

For Kingdom Hall of Jehovah's Witnesses, the Hall on School Street was erected in 1967. Prior to that, the congregation had met in the International Order of Odd Fellows building at 42 Nason Street (the building burned in 1970s, and the present-day occupant of the address is China Ruby restaurant).

St. Stephen's Knanaya Church formed a congregation in 1990 and bought the Main Street building in Maynard in 1992. Previously, the building had been home to "Alku," a Finnish Temperance Society, and then Post No. 1812 of Veterans of Foreign Wars. The Knanaya Church is a house of worship for Knananites, a St. Thomas Christian community whose members trace their ancestry to Syrian Christians who immigrated to India in the year 345.

St. Mary's Indian Orthodox Church began a search for its own place of worship in 1995, completing the purchase of the St. Casimir building from the Roman Catholic Archdiocese of Boston in 2003. The Indian Orthodox Church, also known as the Malankara Orthodox Church, is a faction of the ancient church of the St. Thomas Christians in India. The headquarters of the church is in Kottayam in the Kerala State of southwest India.

The reuse of church buildings as such is problematic, characterized by problems with an aged infrastructure and a question of what uses the main nave and altar space can be put to. Three of Maynard's places of worship were deconsecrated and converted to private residences (St. George's, Evangelical Lutheran and Rodoff Shalom). The Congregational Church building became the performance space The Sanctuary. St. Casimir was sold to St. Mary's Indian Orthodox Church. As of late 2020, the Methodist church building remained empty, and the Mission Evangelical Congregational Church was for sale.

MOVIE THEATERS

The first showing of a motion picture in Maynard was at the Riverside Co-op in 1902. There is also mention of a 1909 exhibition of Sherman's moving pictures at same place. Newspapers of that era mentioned S.E. Sherman as a have-projector-will-travel impresario. By 1914, there were occasional showing of features, shorts and newsreels at Colonial Hall. These were silent films in black-and-white, often accompanied by live music, typically a solo pianist. Intermissions featured performances by local singers.

The first location with regularly scheduled movie showings was Colonial Hall, second story of 65–69 Main Street, in business from 1916 onward. Bartholomew "BJ" Coughlin was one of the owners. Nine cents got you in, and one penny bought candy. Riverside Theatre (then the second floor of what was Gruber Bros. Furniture) started showing movies in 1922, run by Samuel Lerer. Riverside's run ended with a fire in 1934. The Colonial was still in business as late as 1952.

The first building specifically designed to serve as a motion picture palace was Peoples' Theatre. The building still stands at 14 Nason Street, converted to office space. Initially, two groups of local businessmen were scrambling for downtown locations and funding. James A. Coughlan, Hector Hobers and James J. Ledgart organized the Peoples' Theatre Company and sold

The Peoples' Theater building has been rented office space since the 1960s. Back when it was a movie theater, the slogan was "The House of Hits."

shares for twenty-five dollars. The co-operative movement was very strong in Maynard at the time, so the idea of local people being able to buy into ownership and share the profits was well received. In fact, the decision to go for crowd-sourced funding was instrumental to choosing the theater's name.

The second group (with BJ Coughlin, the Naylor brothers and others) had land at the corner of Nason and Main but not quite enough money. The two groups merged. Peoples' Theatre opened on May 6, 1921, with seating for 700 people (250 in the balcony). A huge chandelier graced the lobby. Tickets were twenty-five cents. Around 1951, the price of a ticket went up to forty-four cents for adults and sixteen cents for children. The theater closed its doors after a nearly forty-year run.

Fine Arts Theatre

Although the Coughlans, father James and son Burton, were involved with Peoples' Theatre, Burton decided to build his own theater on the family property at 19 Summer Street. His vision, the luxuriously appointed Fine Arts Theatre, with four hundred seats and no balcony, opened on June 29, 1949, with a showing of *The Red Shoes*. An adjoining second theater, with three hundred seats and its own ticket window, was added in 1969. One employee reminisced, "The projectionist had to scamper across the roof to get to the [projection] booth for the smaller of the theaters." That theater was divided into two parts in 1989.

Over decades, Fine Arts lost its luster (and much of its heat, air conditioning, sound system and waterproofiness) until by the beginnings of this century it was a mess with threadbare carpets, duct-taped seats and sad bathrooms. The Shea family, operating as Deco Entertainment Services, leased the property in late 2002 and started a lengthy rehab process on the interior. Then, in 2013, Burton Coughlan's daughter sold the theater plus the building at 17 Summer Street (originally part of the stables, later Burton's art studio and gallery) to the partnership of Steven Trumble and Melanie Perry.

Their extensive rehabilitation process, outside and inside, required far more money and time than initially expected, including half a year with closed doors and dark screens. Trumble swears that during the remodeling process they excavated and renovated through layers on layers of movie theater detritus, auto body shop and finally down to the wooden timbers, square-cut nails and (rumor had it) a faint aroma of horse manure from

James T. Coughlan opened Coughlan's Livery in 1897, converted the business to an auto shop around 1913 and then, in collaboration with his son, opened the Fine Arts Theatre in 1949. Linda Coughlan Flint, Burton's daughter, sold the theater to Steven Trumble in 2013.

the original horse stable. So it's all the sweeter that sixty-five years after its premiere, the Fine Arts Theatre had a grand reopening in June 2014 with a showing of *Interstellar*. The Theatre Creamery (ice cream) was added in 2020. Concoctions have movie-themed names, such as "Sundae Night Fever."

CO-OPERATIVE SOCIETIES

Maynard's various histories name eight co-operative associations or societies. The oldest was Riverside, and the most recent was Carob Tree. The longest duration and largest was the United Co-operative Society (initially Kaleva Co-operative Association). A Department of Labor report for 1947 mentioned that United was one of the top ten co-ops in the country for oldest, for membership numbers and for annual sales. More than half the households in Maynard were members.

The backstory of co-operatives began in 1844, when a group of 28 working-class men in Rochdale, England, organized the Rochdale Society of Equitable Pioneers and, according to a British Broadcasting Corporation history, "opened their first store, with a small stock of flour, oatmeal, butter, sugar and 24 candles." They soon added tea and tobacco. Their guidelines formed the basis for the principles on which co-operatives around the world continue to operate. The Rochdale Pioneers became highly successful, with 1,400 members by 1855 and 5,560 members by 1870.

There had been earlier attempts to establish co-operatives that were basically buyer's clubs, which, by pooling their purchases, were able to buy at wholesale prices and sell to members at below retail prices. The Rochdale Pioneers were one the early co-operative efforts to add profit-sharing to members based on a percentage of the cost of the goods the members purchased (i.e., a patronage dividend). The seven Rochdale Principles were 1) Open membership, 2) Democratic control, 3) Distribution of surplus (i.e., profits) at end of each year, 4) Interest on capital, 5) Neutrality to religion, race or politics, 6) Cash only and 7) Education programs on co-operative principles. Nonmembers could shop at same prices but did not get the annual members' rebate.

Timeline of Maynard's Co-Operatives

- Order of the Sovereigns of Industry, 1875; became Riverside Co-operative Association in 1878; sold store in 1929; the co-op dissolved after the building burned in 1936
- *Suomalainen Osuuskauppa* (Finnish Co-operative Store), 1899–1900
- Kaleva Co-operative Association, 1907; became United Co-operative Society in 1921 and ended in 1973
- International Co-operative Association, 1911–31
- Maynard Co-operative Milk Association, 1914–17 (merged into Kaleva)
- First National Co-operative Association, 1915–41
- Russian Co-operative Association, 1917–19
- Carob Tree Co-op, 1981–84

Riverside was started by English and Scottish immigrants who worked at the woolen mill. Many of them may have been familiar with the co-operative movement in Great Britain, which by the 1870s had members numbered in the hundreds. Riverside began in 1875 as a chapter in an American movement, the "Order of the Sovereigns of Industry." This was an urban workers organization modeled on the Grange—a farmers' organization formally known as the "Order of Patrons of Husbandry." "Sovereigns" was in effect a buyers' club with intention to secure high-quality goods at lower prices. Locally, this meant buying wholesale in Boston, transporting to Maynard by train and delivering in town by wheelbarrow. Nationally, the Sovereigns organization faltered under financial mismanagement, but in 1878, the local chapter reformed itself as the Riverside Co-Operative Association.

Shares were $5 each (equivalent to about $125 in today's dollars), with members limited to sixty shares. The total capital investment was $1,500. Per the by-laws, regardless of how many shares owned, each shareholder had one vote. The operation started in the basement of the Darling Block building (northeast corner of Summer and Nason Streets), moved to the Riverside Block (later Gruber Bros Furniture) and then in 1882 constructed its own building at the southwest corner of Summer and Nason. The building was a four-story wooden edifice, with the store on the first floor and an entrance on Nason Street. The other floors were rented out.

By 1909, Riverside had more than six hundred members. In addition to quality of goods and competitive prices, members were paid a cash refund twice a year ranging from 2 to 10 percent based on how much shopping they had done and how good a year the co-op was having. Additionally, shares earned 5 percent interest. Decline started with recession of 1920, compounded by cost of repair after a fire the same year. In 1929, the store business was sold to George Morse (the store manager), while the co-op continued to own the building. A fire in 1936 led to dissolution of the association later that year and sale of the site to Knights of Columbus,

The Riverside building was severely damaged by a fire on January 30, 1936. The site was sold to Knights of Columbus, which built a two-story brick building. The Knights sold the building but continue to meet at St. Bridget's. *Courtesy of Maynard Historical Society.*

which had been a longtime tenant. Proceeds were divided among the remaining shareholders.

Contributing factors to the demise were that the children of the founders of Riverside were moving up the socioeconomic ladder at same time as England and Scotland were diminishing as a source of immigrant labor. A front-page newspaper article from 1913 had noted that prior to 1900, the town was mostly English-speaking, but expansion of the mill under new ownership had doubled the town's population by bringing in large numbers of immigrants from Finland, Poland, Lithuania and Italy.

Of the smaller and shorter-lived efforts, *Suomalainen Osuuskauppa* was started 1899 by Finnish immigrants. Capitalized at only $800, it lasted a year before dissolving and selling its store to a private owner. The Maynard Co-operative Milk Association was formed in 1914. Three years later, it became the dairy operations of Kaleva Co-operative Association. Finnish members of the milk co-op who had not wanted to affiliate with the socialist/communist/atheist Kaleva had previously split off and formed the First National Association in late 1915. It owned and operated out of a building on the west corner of Main and River Streets until its demise in 1941. The International Co-operative Association was started in 1911 by immigrants from Poland and lasted twenty years. It began in a building near the Methodist church and later moved to space in the Masonic Building (100–104 Main Street). Membership numbered between two hundred and four hundred over the years. First National and International failed in part because of extending credit to members during the Great Depression. The historical society has a share certificate for the Russian Co-operative Association dated 1917. From details in state records and Concord's newspaper at the time, this effort failed miserably at reaching its capitalization goal of $5,000. Instead, the launch was funded by six men who jointly held a mortgage. It collapsed two years later when the mortgagees decided to liquidate the operation, selling the goods and fixtures at auction.

From Kaleva to United

"Kaleva" refers to an ancient, mythological Finnish ruler known from a nineteenth-century work of epic poetry and storytelling compiled by folklorist researcher Elias Lonnrot. The work, the *Kalevala*, is regarded as the national epic of Finland, instrumental in fostering a sense of Finnish national identity that culminated in the Finnish declaration of

The Kaleva Co-operative Association started in 1907 in rented space. This 1915 photo shows employees in front of the building (now 54–58 Main). *Courtesy of Maynard Historical Society.*

independence from Russian rule in 1917. Locally, immigrants had formed the Finnish Workingmen's Socialist Society in 1903, from whom the 187 founders of the co-operative were drawn.

According to the book *The Finnish Imprint*, a delegation of Finnish immigrants had initially approached the large and prospering Riverside Co-operative Association with the idea of becoming members. Because many of the recent immigrants did not speak English, they asked that the co-operative hire Finnish store clerks. This suggestion was rebuffed, with a reply that if they did not like the service they received, they should start their own store. They did. The business was initially capitalized at $1,600 from sale of 320 shares at $5 per share (equivalent to about $125 in 2020 dollars). The initial location was a rented storefront on Main Street. By 1912, the co-operative had bought the entire two-story building and soon after added a bakery operation, a dairy with home delivery and a restaurant on the second floor, serving meals to hundreds of workers living in neighboring boardinghouses.

Maynard was not the only home to a Finnish-organized co-operative. Fitchburg has the Into Co-operative and Quincy the Turva Co-operative. In 1919, Maynard, these two and others merged to create the United Co-operative Society of New England. This was short-lived due to financial and political disagreements, the end result being that the Maynard group reorganized as the United Co-operative Society of Maynard and Fitchburg became the United Co-operative Society of Fitchburg. The latter was the last of the Finnish co-operatives to close their doors, in 1977.

United's by-laws had added an eighth principle to the previously described Rochdale seven: continuous expansion. Over the initial fifty years, membership grew from 184 to 2,960 as coal and firewood (1924), fuel oil (1933) and ice (1934) deliveries were added. In addition to the Main Street store, a branch store was opened on the northeast corner of Waltham and Powdermill Roads (1926), superseded by moving the branch store operations to a new building at the northwest corner of the same intersection (1936). This remained active until it was sold to Murphy and Snyder printers in 1957. Next door, now the 7-Eleven/Dunkin' Donuts store, was an automobile gas and service station (1934).

A report by the U.S. Bureau of Labor at that time stated that the United Co-operative Society of Maynard was one of the ten largest in the country, calculated either by number of members or annual sales, and that it was also one of the ten oldest. More than half the households in Maynard belonged to United. At its peak, the co-operative had more than fifty full-time employees, with medical benefits and life insurance—unusual for that era.

United survived the competition from an A&P supermarket operating on Nason Street (in the building now housing the Outdoor Store), but the presence of Victory Supermarket on Powdermill Road, combined with the freedom to shop for food elsewhere provided by increased car ownership, put pressure on the co-operative. In June 1973, there was a vote held to dissolve—votes in favor were 97 percent. United's by-laws had an interesting clause: on the occasion of dissolution, which required a three-fourths majority of votes at a meeting, the assets would be used to pay the purchase value of the outstanding shares. As a disincentive to taking this action, any surplus would go to the Co-operative League of the United States rather than to members.

In 1981, a natural foods effort named the Carob Tree Co-op was started in Concord by Debra Stark. It later moved to Acton and then Maynard, where it occupied a small store on River Street; it later went back to Acton. In addition to paid staff, the close to 150 members took turns volunteering at the store. It closed after several years. Debra Stark went on to start Debra's Natural Gourmet, in West Concord, in 1989.

Children of United Co-op members waiting for the bus to take them to summer day camp at Vose Pond. They are in front of the co-op building at Parker and Waltham that was sold to Murphy & Snyder Printers in 1957. *Courtesy of Maynard Historical Society.*

And now, well into the twenty-first century, there is an effort underway to launch Assabet Co-op Market. The beginnings date to February 2012, when a small group of people met to discuss forming a co-op. The cost of membership was set at $200. As of late 2020, more than 1,300 people have joined. The near-term goal is to find and commit to a retail space on the order of 6,000 square feet, with immediately adjacent parking. Once a site is identified, there will be fundraising effort to reach the capitalization goal of about $4.6 million, hopefully achieved via a combination of local and state grants, bank loans and interest-paying loans from members. Capitalization is expected to take four to six months. Once launched, Assabet Co-op Market intends to make a point of sourcing food from local farms. If all goes as planned, Maynard will once again be a co-operative town, 145 years after the start of the first.

Chapter 7

MAYNARD BOOMS AND BUSTS

Maynard cycled through the highs and lows of being a one-company town. When the woolen mill started production in 1847, the hamlet known as Assabet Village was home to a modest-sized paper mill and a gunpowder manufacture operation on the east side. The woolen mill grew to employ thousands, and the town grew with it, becoming a transportation hub (train and electric trolley) and a commercial center with hotels and stores. The town crashed when the mill did, a pattern repeated when Digital Equipment Corporation closed its doors and again when Clock Tower Place faltered, after having lost Monster.com, its largest tenant. To some degree, the adage "As goes the mill, so goes Maynard" still applies.

WOOL MILL BOOMS AND BUSTS, 1846–1950

Factory towns go through boom and bust cycles. Maynard was no exception. The woolen mill operations that dominated the town for more than one hundred years began in 1846 under Amory Maynard and William Knight in a single wooden building, one hundred by fifty feet, producing wool yarn and carpet in 1847, incorporated as Assabet Manufacturing Company in 1849. The simple (read: oft-repeated) story is that the mill failed in 1857 as a consequence of the Panic of 1857 and restarted in 1862. The truth appears more complex. Shortly after incorporation, Knight sold his mill interests to Maynard, with the majority of the sale price of $50,000 as a mortgage. Knight—who had moved from Framingham to Boston, never living in Assabet Village—continued to own other land and buildings. Mill operations did stop in 1857, but Amory retained full ownership and was not insolvent; in 1858, he bought water rights to Fort Meadow Pond, Marlborough, for $8,000 as a water supply contributor to his mill.

In 1861, the mill failed. The probate court judge directed the assignees to sell Mr. Maynard's mill properties in conjunction with William H. Knight the mortgagee. On October 14, the properties were sold to George H. Preston for $71,000 (paying off Knight's mortgage). The deed was signed October 26, 1861. T. Quincy Browne, one of the assignees of the Maynard estate, purchased Mr. Knight's other land and buildings in Stow, Sudbury and Marlborough on November 30, 1861, for $75,000.

On September 10, 1862, the Assabet Manufacturing Company was reincorporated with a capital of $200,000 for the purpose of manufacturing cotton, wool, flax and silk in the towns of Stow and Sudbury. The officers of the corporation were Thomas A. Goddard, president; T. Quincy Browne, treasurer; and Amory Maynard, agent. On September 30, 1862, T. Quincy Browne sold the property he purchased from William H. Knight to the Assabet Manufacturing Company for $100,000. The net effect here was that William Knight was completely bought out—possibly at below-market prices—and the business was reincorporated a year later with Amory Maynard as a minority owner. The manufacture of French flannels and dress goods was substituted for carpets.

Amory owned 20 percent of the shares. Lorenzo Maynard, Amory's son, was second in command as superintendent. Separate from the mill, Amory owned extensive property in Assabet Village. A&L Maynard (a company named after Amory and Lorenzo) was created as a landholding and construction company, building commercial buildings, boardinghouses and homes.

The impetus for starting up again in 1862 was in part to meet Union army demands for blankets and other woolen goods (some histories say cloth for uniforms) for the Civil War. The first brick building was erected in about 1862, a structure 170 by 50 feet, six stories high, placed over the original wooden building so that manufacturing continued uninterrupted. In 1866, a mill 124 by 70 feet and four stories high was erected; in 1868, another building was added, 157 by 50 feet and four stories high. More buildings were added 1872 and 1892.

Sewing room employees at the Assabet Woolen Company, 1904. *Courtesy of Maynard Historical Society.*

In 1898, the mill complex, still operating under the name Assabet Manufacturing Company, with Amory's son Lorenzo as agent, failed again. It was not entirely Lorenzo's fault. In 1894, the federal government ended protective tariffs on wool cloth entering the country as part of the Wilson-Gorman Tariff Act. Dozens of U.S. wool mills went under. The Dingley Act of 1897 restored the protective tariff, but it was too late for Maynard. In 1899, the American Woolen Company (AWC), a huge multi-state operation, bought the mill on the cheap. Over time, AWC added the three large buildings facing the millpond and switched to coal for power and coal gas for illumination (later using electric lights).

Throughout the first half of the twentieth century, labor unrest periodically closed the mill for short periods of time. In 1903, there was unrest for a raise from $10.44 per week ($5 per hour in 2020 inflation-adjusted dollars). In 1914, workers went on strike for a shortening of the fifty-four-hour workweek.

The Great Depression put everyone on short workweeks and then closed the mill entirely in 1931. Production slowly recovered during the latter half of the '30s and then for World War II was operating around the clock, seven days a week, on military contracts for blankets and cloth for winter coats. After the war, it limped on until 1950. The American Woolen Company had blanket and wool cloth government contracts for the Korean War, but it filled those at other sites. When the woolen mill closed after 104 years, Maynard was quiet to the point that kids could play hopscotch on Main Street.

MAYNARD INDUSTRIES INCORPORATED, 1953–1974

A group of local business people tried to arrange financing to buy the property in 1950, but that failed. It was not until July 1953 that a group from Worcester, Maynard Industries Incorporated (MII), closed a deal. What the group bought was 1.2 million square feet of brick and wooden buildings; the land also included the millpond, the Ben Smith Dam, Lake Boon and part of Fort Meadow Reservoir. The purchase price of $200,000 equates to $1.9 million in today's dollars. A bargain! A few years later, Lake Boon was relinquished to the Town of Stow in lieu of unpaid property taxes, and Fort Meadow was sold to Marlborough.

Irving Burg was hired to be the facilities manager six months after the purchase. His credentials were bachelor's and master's degrees in education, a stint in the U.S. Army during World War II and several years managing a textile plant. His job was to keep the place running and rent out all the space. By April 1954, the mill was 50 percent rented and by November, 70 percent. Despite desperately necessary facility improvements, the operation was profitable by the third year and every year thereafter until Digital Equipment Corporation (DEC), a tenant starting in 1957, bought the entire complex (including millpond, canal and dam) in July 1974. Burg's history of the mill complex, written in 1982, mentions that in his twenty-one years as manager, the mill had eighty-two companies as tenants. Among the many were Bradley Container Corporation, Dennison Manufacturing, Raytheon and more.

Berg's recollections returned again and again to parking problems. One has to realize that during the complex's decades as a woolen mill, employees walked to work. Dennison Manufacturing—in the giftwrap paper business—finally insisted on a dedicated lot, so fill was added next to Main Street, making space for one hundred cars. Years later, more parking needed, so one of the two chimneys was demolished and the bricks were added to the fill. This widened the parking lot that now hosts the farmers' market. DEC, needing parking for Building 5, accomplished this by filling in more of the pond on the south side.

Here's another parking story. Into the '60s, space was so tight that people were allowed to park in the mill yard on the railroad tracks. For the infrequent arrivals of a freight train on the spur that ran into the mill, all cars had to be moved. Burg had everyone's phone number. He and his secretary would hastily get on the phones. Whenever the call came, Ken Olsen, president of DEC, would step out of his office to move his car.

FROM DIGITAL TO FRANKLIN LIFECARE TO CLOCK TOWER PLACE

Digital Equipment Corporation's ownership of the mill complex spanned from July 1974 to November 1994. Downsizing worldwide started in January 1991. All of Digital's operations in the mill buildings shut down in 1993. In November 1994, Digital sold the mill to a newly formed healthcare company called Franklin Lifecare Corporation (FLC). The price was $1.5 million. It was a fire sale; during DEC's last year, the town had assessed the value of the mill at $25 million and set property taxes at $671,000. Digital was not completely out of the facility. The Maynard Historical Society has correspondence about DEC leasing space from Franklin, as well as disputes about whether equipment was DEC's to sell or had been part of the sale.

FLC's plans were described in a prospectus titled "Mill Pond Village." The intent was to start by finding commercial tenants for Buildings 1 and 3, facing the millpond. The follow-up was to create a massive senior independent living, assisted living and nursing home complex in the other buildings. The project was to have up to eight hundred living units, dining rooms, craft rooms, a museum for the town (!) and a café overlooking the Assabet River. Funding never materialized. Franklin went into foreclosure. The mill complex stayed mostly vacant until Wellesley Rosewood Capital LLC (Clock Tower Place, CTP) agreed to buy it in October 1997, closing the deal on January 1, 1998.

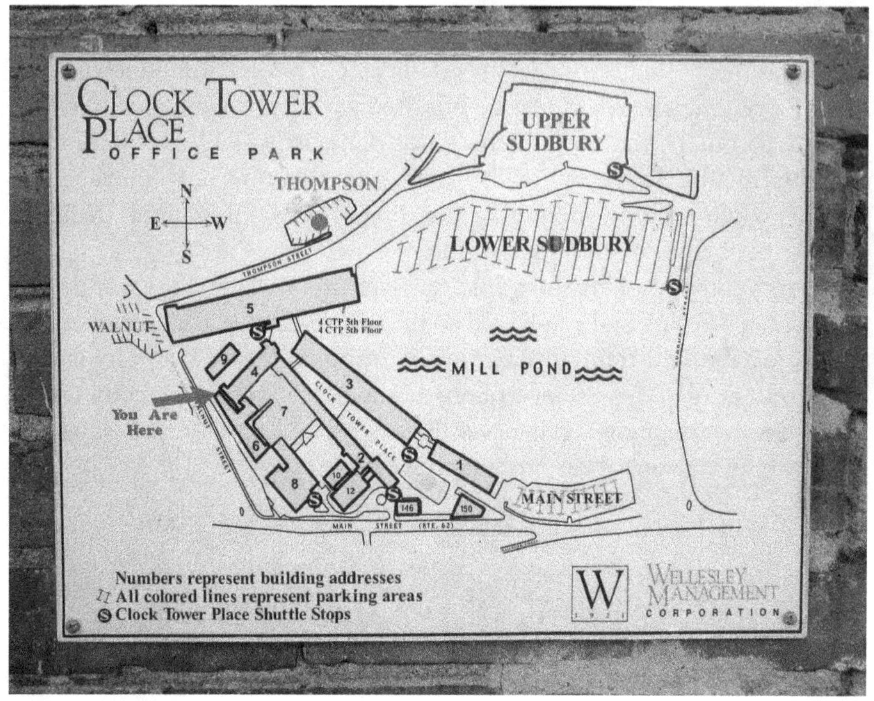

This Clock Tower Place map shows building numbering circa 1998–2015; Mill & Main demolished no. 10 and part of no. 2 and did some renumbering. The compass rose reversed north and south.

An essential part of the deal for Clock Tower Place was an agreement with the Town of Maynard establishing tax incentive financing (TIF). The terms were that for increases in assessed value of the property—based on improvements to the buildings and grounds and increased value as tenants moved in—there would be a 95 percent discount of property taxes for the first five years and a 50 percent discount for the following ten years. The TIF was approved at a town meeting in April 1998 and was to run from July 1998 through June 2013. The TIF initially saved CTP more than $500,000 per year. CTP also got a state abandoned building tax credit. Because of the tax breaks, Clock Tower Place was able to offer below-market rental rates. By mid-1999, the mill complex was at 50 percent occupancy; the following February, it was at 73 percent; and by the end of 2000, it was full.

CLOCK TOWER PLACE TO MILL & MAIN

For signage styling, Mill & Main opted for "mill&main," with white lettering on an orange background.

After filling the existing buildings with tenants, CTP was so optimistic about potential growth that it proposed adding a new 300,000-square-foot building on the south side of the millpond plus a five-story parking garage. Then, the business outlook changed. Three years into the recession that had started in 2008, the vacancy rate was hovering around 30 percent, with more departures expected. The death knell sounded when Monster.com relocated. This international job-search company had moved to CTP in 1998 with about 50,000 square feet of floor space. Within years it had expanded to 300,000 square feet. Monster also had a visible presence in town, sponsoring blood drives and an annual road race to benefit the Boys & Girls Club of Assabet Valley. In early 2014, the company, which had already been downsizing (having missed the social media impact on job search that had fostered LinkedIn), relocated all of its more than six hundred remaining employees to Weston.

With Monster gone, Wellesley Rosewood was facing less than 30 percent occupancy, a $50 million mortgage and an expired TIF. Clock Tower Place was put up for sale. The buyers, in 2015, were Artemis Real Estate Partners and Saracen Properties, having bought the mortgage and secured an additional $40.8 million financing. The mill complex was rebranded as Mill & Main. Lincoln Property Company was brought in as on-site managers. Remodeling included removal of two of the smaller buildings (no. 10 and part of no. 2) and extensive landscaping. Town-approved zoning changes allowed for residential, retail and restaurant opportunities. Heading toward Maynard's 150th anniversary, Mill & Main continues to seek tenants for the building space and other options that could benefit it and the town.

Chapter 8

DIGITAL EQUIPMENT CORPORATION

Someone, somewhere, is making a product that will make your product obsolete.
—Georges Doriot

Georges Doriot headed the venture capital group that provided initial funding to Digital Equipment Corporation (DEC). Minicomputers—Digital's *raison d'être*—did not quite make mainframe computers obsolete, but the rise of desktop and laptop computers linked to servers were part of the death knell for DEC. While it existed, DEC elicited extreme employee loyalty due to empowerment stemming from its novel matrix management system.

DEC'S ORIGIN, RISE AND STATUS AS A WORLD LEADER

Origin

The rise and fall of Digital Equipment Corporation was a forty-one-year arc that started with a bit of rented space in the mill buildings on July 9, 1957, and peaked in size and sales in 1990 with the mill complex being the world headquarters of a 125,000-employee empire that reached $14 billion in annual sales. Then, as a result of management and technology missteps, the company repeatedly downsized, had a fire sale of assets and was finally sold to Compaq Corporation in 1998.

In the beginning, there was the Massachusetts Institute of Technology (MIT). Kenneth "Ken" Olsen, born in 1926, had done a stint in the navy right out of high school and then attended MIT as undergraduate and graduate student, completing a master's degree in electrical engineering in 1952. After graduating, Olsen started a job at Lincoln Laboratory, a MIT-affiliated facility focused on military research. It was at Lincoln Labs that the first transitions were made from vacuum tubes to transistor-based computers. Olsen oversaw the development of a machine called the TX-0. Much of the design, though improved, was incorporated into DEC's first computers.

In May 1957, Olsen and Harlan Anderson, a colleague at Lincoln Labs, approached a venture capitalist company with a proposal for a "digital computer corporation." They got an investment of $70,000 for a 70 percent share in the company. There was pushback from the investors about "Computer" being in the company's name, because at the time computers were large, expensive, mostly unprofitable machines—think IBM and UNIVAC—and hence the name became Digital Equipment Corporation.

In 1957, the mill complex was almost entirely rented out to dozens of businesses. Only because of a timely bankruptcy of a small company did space happen to open up when Olsen and Andersen first came calling on July 9. After a few visits, they signed a three-year lease on August 27 for 8,680 square feet at $300 per month. They and Stan Olsen, Ken's younger brother (employee number three), spent days painting the space themselves. They also went to Gruber Bros. Furniture and bought $69 worth of office furniture—on thirty days' credit.

For the first three years, they were profitably producing electronic test modules for engineering laboratories and, in the meantime, working on Digital's first computer, the PDP-1. By October 1961, the company had grown to 265 employees, and annual sales were approaching $6 million. In time, DEC made Maynard the "Minicomputer Capital of the World."

There is a great story of how Ken pursued his wife. On vacation from MIT and visiting his parents in Connecticut, he was smitten with a woman, Aulikki Valve (full name: Eeva-Liisa Aulikki Valve), from Finland, who was staying with neighbors. Nothing came of it at the time, but after she returned to Finland and he to MIT, he could not stop thinking about her. Olsen wrote a letter, asking if he might visit. Her reply? "Don't bother." Not taking no for an answer, he took a leave of absence from MIT, took a ship to Europe, bicycled to Denmark and then ferried to Sweden, where he got a job as an electrician at a ball bearing factory. This journey was perhaps not entirely crazy. His mother's parents had come from Sweden (and his father's parents from Norway), so it is possible that he had relatives there.

Once settled in, Olsen wrote to Aulikki again. This time, she agreed to see him. Olsen quit his job, traveled to Finland, arrived at Aulikki's parents' house and proposed marriage. The response was "No," from both Aulikki and her parents. Did Olsen return to the United States? No. He continued to court Aulikki. After two months, the answer became "Yes." They married, in Finland, and then returned to Massachusetts, where he competed his graduate degree.

Olsen had always said that the reasons he started the company in Maynard included the low rent and the availability of an under-employed, factory-skilled workforce, but an unmentioned reason might have been the presence of a Finnish-speaking population, to help his wife be a bit less homesick. Although the Olsens lived in Lincoln, there are many mentions of Aulikki and their three children visiting Ken at the mill. Aulikki died in 2009 after fifty-nine years of marriage. Ken passed two years later.

Rise

Among the many stories Ken Olsen told about the early years was how primitive the working conditions were. Workspaces had walls but no doors. In the summer, with no air conditioning, windows were opened but there were no screens, so the work area was plagued by pigeons. In the depths of winter, the heat was constantly on, but during the spring and fall, it was off on weekends. Raytheon shared one building with Digital's space. If Raytheon wanted weekend heat, Digital got heat. Raytheon would call at noon on Friday to specify which buildings it wanted heated, paying fifteen dollars per hour for the service. Ken Olsen would call at 1:00 p.m. to see if he was going to get his part of the building heated for free.

The early successes of DEC rested on two concepts: real time computing and time sharing. The first described the ability to sit in front of a computer, create program code on a keyboard and see code and output on a video screen. The second referred to the idea that more than one user could be using the same computer at the same time, with speed fast enough that each user had the sense that he or she was the sole operator.

The PDP-1 was DEC's first computer, introduced in December 1959. The first delivery to a customer was in November 1960. It introduced the concept of real-time computing. It weighed about 1,600 pounds, sold for $30,000 (roughly $1 million in inflation-adjusted dollars) and was considered a huge bargain compared to mainframe computers. DEC sold fifty-three of them. One was on permanent loan to the Massachusetts Institute of Technology Electrical Engineering Department, Ken Olsen's alma mater, where faculty and students could sign up for computer time, 24/7. DEC recruited students who showed promise.

As to where "PDP" came from, Olsen, in a 1988 interview, mentioned that one of the first potential customers for their first computer was the U.S. Geological Survey, for earthquake research, but Congress had decreed that no agency could purchase a computer until all the computers the government already owned were 100 percent in use. So Digital, already being in the "Equipment" business rather than the computer business, decided to call its first model a Programmed Data Processor. Hence, "PDP-1."

The PDP-8, introduced in 1965, became DEC's first superstar minicomputer, selling more than fifty thousand units over its life span. The innovative idea—radical at the time—was to make a smaller, cost-effective computer rather than going for "bigger equals better." There had been prior missteps. PDP models 4 through 7 were sluggish sellers, and the PDP-6 in particular had devoured huge amounts of the company's research and development budget. The PDP-8 supported time-sharing, meaning that many people could be using terminals at the same time but have the response time they expected from being the only user of a real-time computer. The introductory price was $18,500.

The original PDP-8 spawned a large family of models that were progressively smaller, faster and less expensive. One anecdote of the time was that Bob Metcalf, a graduate student at MIT, had received permission to have a PDP-8 on loan in his office for a weekend demonstration for visiting high school students. When he got to his office that Saturday, the computer was gone. DEC's public relations department turned the crime into an advertising coup, describing the PDP-8 as "The first computer small enough to steal." Metcalf went on to co-invent the Ethernet, parent concept for the Internet. The PDP-8 system was later incorporated into one of DEC's entries into the personal computer niche: the DECmate II/III.

Financially, a major milestone was achieved when the company issued stock on August 18, 1966, at an initial public offering of 375,000 shares at $22/share, raising a bit over $8 million for about 20 percent of the company (the majority of shares retained by the investor). Given that the company had been initially funded by $70,000 from American Research & Development, one of the first venture capital companies in the United

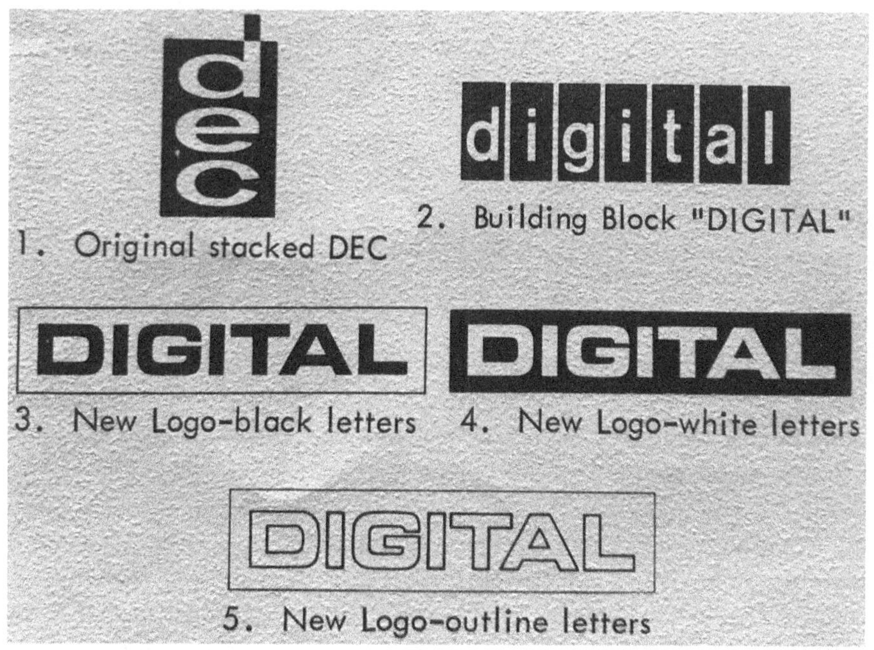

Digital's logo went through several evolutions, starting as vertically stacked "dec" and then a horizontal "digital," with each letter in its own block. In 1965, briefly, it was all capital letters. Each PDP model had its own color for the blocks, but with introduction of the VAX line in late 1977, everything was "Digital Blue." Ten years later, the background color was changed to burgundy, perhaps to avoid confusion with IBM having become nicknamed "Big Blue." Finally, in 1993, during the layoffs era, square dots over the letter *i* became circles, and the ends of the letters *g*, *t* and *a* were slanted rather than horizontal. This did not save the company. *Courtesy of Maynard Historical Society.*

States, for 70 percent ownership, this achievement was insanely profitable for AR&D. Harlan Anderson, one of the cofounders, later wrote, "This deal seems ridiculous and unfair by today's standards; however, we never contacted an alternative source of capital. We were very naïve and there was very little venture capital money available then. We accepted the offer without any negotiation." When AR&D was purchased in 1972, the price was $450 million; the major asset in its portfolio was Digital.

The PDP-11 reached the market in 1970. DEC had ended up behind IBM and Data General—the latter started in Hudson by ex-DEC engineers. DEC "bet the farm" on leapfrogging the competition. It succeeded. Various versions in the PDP-11 family sold more than 600,000 computers to all corners of the world. The need to fulfill sales and service contracts on this vast family meant that DEC needed to have thousands of employees in scores of countries. The PDP-11 models had a successful twenty-year run, until being rendered obsolete by microcomputers connected to server networks.

Prior to the Soviet Union invading Afghanistan in 1979 and a subsequent boycott on importing U.S. computers, PDP-8s and PDP-11s legally made their way behind the Iron Curtain. There they were reverse-engineered to create knock-offs. Some were so compatible that they could run DEC software, and a DEC sales force in eastern Europe reported seeing Russian-language PDP manuals. Years later, VAX machines were smuggled into the USSR and cloned as "WAX" superminicomputers, also able to run DEC software. There is a confirmed story that the scribe panel of the Digital CVAX microprocessor had text in the Cyrillic (Russian) alphabet, with one suggested translation as, "VAX—when you care enough to steal the very best." This was actually a rift on the famous Hallmark card slogan, "When you care enough to send the best."

Minicomputer Capital of the World

Harlan Anderson, cofounder, left the company in 1966. Anderson's memoir described the problem as a major difference in his and Olsen's visions for how to manage the fast-growing company. Anderson favored a traditional hierarchy. Olsen, having put in a bit over a year in Poughkeepsie, New York, as MIT's liaison to IBM, loathed that type of rigidity. Each had his champions on the board of directors, respectively Jay Forrester, who had been their boss at Lincoln Labs, later a professor at the MIT Sloan School of Management, and Georges Doriot, president of the venture capital firm that had provided startup funding for DEC.

Anderson's position within the company had been weakened by his ties to the failed PDP-6 computer. He resigned rather than assume a lesser position. Forrester left the board soon thereafter. Doriot stayed on into the late 1980s. Olsen went on to commit to a matrix-style management that perplexed business school academics for years yet seemed to work fine for a company of engineers making leading-edge products for engineers.

DEC dominated the minicomputer niche. In 1971, Massachusetts governor Francis William Sargent declared Maynard the "Minicomputer Capital of the World." By then, DEC had expanded to renting most of the mill. One year later, it bought the sixty-acre Parker Street industrial complex. In 1974, it bought the entire mill complex and, in time, a few other buildings in town, bringing the total to more than 2 million square

DEC's need for parking lots led to the shrinking of the millpond. *Courtesy of Maynard Historical Society.*

feet of office and factory space. A townwide celebration of DEC's twenty-fifth anniversary—and DEC's restoration of the ninety-year-old clock tower—took place in 1983.

Exact numbers are not available, but estimates are that Digital employed between one-third and one-half of the adults living in Maynard. Students were hired right out of high school. Other employees commuted—Routes 117 and 27 had twice daily traffic jams, and the millpond was partially filled in to create more parking. Restaurants and bars were flooded with employees most evenings. There were no empty storefronts. Was there a downside? Yes, in that Maynard was once again a one-company town.

VAX was Digital's second act. The name choice itself was significant, as after almost twenty years of "PDP-next," this was a whole new system. The acronym stood for "Virtual Address Extension." Design and development started in 1975. The VAX-11/780 was introduced in October 1977. In tech-speak, VAX had a novel instruction set architecture incorporating a 32-bit system. According to the Wikipedia article on VAX, its primary features were "its very large number of assembly-language-programmer-friendly addressing modes and machine instructions, highly orthogonal architecture, and instructions for complex operations such as queue insertion or deletion and polynomial evaluation." In non-tech-speak, the VAX computer systems were flexible, robust and scalable. As a customer's information technology needs grew, more VAX machines could be added and networked through a new means: the Ethernet. New VAX models were introduced well into the early 1990s, but everything remained compatible.

There was a downside. Faced with an internal competition for resources, Ken Olsen decided in 1982 that it was time to kill the extremely successful PDP-11 series. Vice Presidents Rose Anne Giordano and Winston "Win" Hindle were tasked with the announcement at the annual DECUS symposium. The sense of betrayal led some clients to abandon DEC, but most transitioned to VAX. It helped that DEC sweetened the pot with discounts. The success of VAX catapulted DEC into higher and higher income levels: $1.0 billion for 1977, $4.0 billion for 1982 and $11.4 billion for 1988.

DEC's market capitalization—number of shares times price per share—reached a peak of $24 billion in 1987. The company was riding the peak of the "bet the farm" introduction of the VAX-based minicomputers a decade earlier. Even though it had stumbled badly in beginnings of the microcomputer era, DEC had a valid claim to being the second-largest computer company in the world. What DEC did not see coming was changes embodied by the famous quote by Georges Doriot: "Someone, somewhere, is making a product that will make your product obsolete."

"TO PC OR NOT PC" AND DEC'S DECLINE

Personal Computers

Olsen was correctly quoted but misunderstood when in a talk given to a 1977 World Future Society meeting in Boston, he said, "There is no reason for any individual to have a computer in their home." This statement was repeated in *TIME* magazine and elsewhere. Keep in mind that the first non-hobbyist "personal computers," including the Apple II, reached the market in 1977, with the IBM PC appearing in 1981.

In the full context of Ken's talk, he was a nonbeliever in the futuristic idea that we would turn over to computers the day-to-day operations of our homes—such as paying bills, turning lights and heat on and off, running security systems, keeping inventory of food supplies in the house and creating a shopping list accordingly (and yet, here we are). Ken also knew that computers were evolving so rapidly that any purchased home computer would soon become obsolete. (So true!) In his mind, the proper solution was to have video screens, keyboards and printers in homes and at businesses, all linked electronically to company-operated computers that would provide the software, software upgrades and memory. DEC actually launched the first of what became a series of video terminals in 1974 as the VT50, followed by VT52 and then the VT100 in 1978; they were superseded in time by VT200, VT300, VT400 and VT500. Collectively, the VT line sold more than 6 million units.

As to desktop computers, over decades, DEC had committed itself to selling midsize computers that generated significant profits by customizing software and providing service. A leap to also making low-priced, low-profit, small computers that would run software provided by other companies saved IBM but stymied Digital. Only after IBM launched personal computers in August 1981 did DEC decide to enter the fray. It initiated three separate PC projects at separate company facilities, with poor communication among them. DEC's standard procedure would have been to then decide which was best and kill the other two. Instead, all three were brought to market (perhaps overly quickly) in 1982: the high-end Professional, the DECmate series (offering only word processing) and the more general-purpose Rainbow 100.

DEC being DEC, everything was of high quality and ran various versions of DEC's software, but by not being open to the flood of software that IBM was allowing all companies to make to run on its machines, DEC failed to set the standard and did not follow the standard. Even for something as simple as floppy disks, DEC used its own proprietary formatting. And as a consequence of poor internal communications and DEC's bias toward proprietary systems, its three microcomputers were also not compatible with one another.

As an example of the problems, DEC did not have a marketing, sales and delivery system that could put its PCs into stores or else sell and deliver directly to consumers. PCs did not require the lucrative support and service contracts that followed placement of minicomputers. And finally, as one sales person put it, "Why try to sell 12 Rainbows when you can get the same commission on selling just one VAX?"

A few years later, a proposal emerged from the Engineering Department to start over, but this time with competitively priced clones of the IBM system, able to run all the software that was making the IBM PCs so successful for business applications. Compaq and Dell had already jumped into this niche. DEC was already doing cost-effective mass production of desktop systems as video terminals. All it would take was to turn out a sturdy, fast, high-end clone. Ken Olsen killed the proposal. His attitude was that Digital was a leader, not a follower.

By the time Olsen reversed himself on this topic, in 1991, it was too late. DEC brought out a series of high-end, extremely reliable, IBM-compatible machines. But Compaq, Dell, Gateway, HP and others had a much larger share of what was transitioning to a low-profit-margin business. When merger talks first started with Compaq, Digital was manufacturing about 1 million PCs per year. Compaq was doing twelve times that number.

DEC's Decline and Fall

After protracted negotiations, Compaq agreed to acquire a downsized Digital Equipment Corporation in January 1998. The deal closed in June. The purchase price was $9.6 billion. This for a computer company once second only to IBM, a company that had reached annual sales of $14 billion, market capitalization of $24 billion and 125,000 employees working in more than eighty countries.

Stumbles in the end that contributed to DEC's decline and fall were many. A simplistic, oft-repeated story is that DEC had declined to get into the personal computer business, but this was only a small part of the problem. Circa 1985, DEC decided to compete in the arena of commercial data centers. This market traditionally belonged to IBM, and to complete would require a massive increase in staff involved in sales and service. The employee population increased by 26,800 in two years. Around the same time, senior management decided that the upgraded VAX system would no longer support "open architecture," making it difficult for manufacturers of add-on components. DEC also decided that any purchase of a used DEC computer would require a fee to relicense the software that was already on the computer. Profitable short-term? Yes. Angry customers? Also yes.

The company was also strongly committed to vertical integration, meaning that it wanted to own its manufacture of components—chips, screens, keyboards—even when buying from independent companies would cost less. Meanwhile, competition had gained ground. Sun Microsystems and Data General competed head to head in the minicomputer niche; DEC failed in an attempt to compete with IBM in the mainframe niche. Development of the failed VAX9000 mainframe chewed through $3 billion in critically needed capital. And while DEC was focusing upward on IBM, all the microcomputer companies were approaching fast from below.

DEC's crash was fast. President Ken Olsen, sixty-five years old in 1991, was strongly against layoffs. In a May 1992 article in the *New York Times*, he noted, "We've lived through many recessions. This is just one more." The last year of billion-dollar profits was 1989. Total revenue continued to increase, but 1990 was only marginally profitable and subsequent years saw losses in the hundreds of millions of dollars. Restructuring was rampant and continuous. People in senior management were leaving. There were hiring freezes, followed by offerings of early retirement and generous severance packages for those willing to volunteer to leave. The layoffs began in earnest in January 1991, including in Maynard. All company operations in the mill buildings shut down in 1993, with layoffs or relocations of 2,100 employees. The Parker Street complex closed soon after. Company headquarters were relocated to a new building on Powdermill Road (later sold to Stratus Technologies).

The company had weathered downturns before by depending on its research excellence to leapfrog the competition to a new industry supremacy. This time, that would not be the case. In July 1992, the company's board of directors forced Olsen to resign. For thousands of employees, working for DEC within the empowering management system and mantra of "Do the right thing," this was a heart-wrenching event. A forum comment from one employee read, "I used to drive to the office in the morning, and I couldn't wait to get to work—I love my job and the company environment….The company doesn't love itself anymore. Now I drive to work in the morning and all I can think about is getting out of this company and doing something else."

Robert Palmer, who had joined the company in 1985 to run the computer chip manufacturing division, took over as president, also taking on the title of chief executive officer and later chairman of the board. He was perceived as competent but not visionary. Over six years, Palmer oversaw plant closings, staff relocations, layoffs of sixty thousand employees and sale of many of the major components of the company. Downsizing cost the company close to $5 billion in layoffs and facility closings.

Even during the decline, there had been successes. Digital launched the Internet search engine AltaVista in 1995. It was the most popular among many competing search engines such as Lycos, AskJeeves and Yahoo! until Google came to dominate the market after 2000. According to one source, Larry Page and Sergey Brin had approached DEC in 1997 with their Pagerank system, hoping to be acquired by AltaVista, before going on to start Google.

DEC was not alone in suffering setbacks and contractions in the 1990s. IBM shrank from 405,000 employees in 1985 to 220,000 by 1994 and reduced its stock dividend by two-thirds. Data General, Wang Laboratories, Prime Computer, Lotus Development Corporation and Apollo Computer were all Greater Boston computer companies that faded and folded or were acquired around the same time.

Was the sale inevitable? Probably not. With a different senior management, it is possible that Digital could have survived, perhaps prospered, but it is unlikely that it could have regained its aura as a radically innovative company attracting the best and the brightest.

WOMEN AND MINORITIES AT DEC

Ken Olsen was a big believer in numbers. Employees were assigned consecutive numbers based on order of hire, later becoming their badge numbers. Ken was no. 1, and Harlan was no. 2. The first two women hired were Alma E. Pontz, no. 5, and Gloria Porrazzo, no. 6. Barbara Stephenson was no. 71. One thing about badge numbers: your badge number became yours and was retired when you left the company. Employees returning after a gap in service could apply for "their" old number back.

Women were not rare at Digital. From perusing a list of the first one hudred full-time employees, thirty-six were women. Years later, the main reasons Olsen gave for locating in Maynard were low rent and a local workforce with lots of factory experience. Many of the women were walk-to-work Maynardites, some of whom had worked in the same buildings in the woolen mill era, which had ended less than ten years back. The newly refurbished work areas were clean, quiet and well lit, although they were hot during the summers, as air conditioning was not installed until around 1970.

Alma E. Pontz was the first woman hired. According to her 2013 obituary, she had already put in twenty-four years in the wool business before being hired by Olsen as the first administrative assistant. She was more than a decade older than her bosses. She stayed with DEC until she retired twenty-one years later.

Gloria Porrazzo was the first woman hired to work in assembling Laboratory Modules and Systems Modules. These products allowed Digital to be profitable from its first year onward. According to Peter Koch, plant manager, Porrazzo stayed with the company for twenty-five years, rising to the level of production manager. The fifty to sixty women who worked for her in Assembly were informally known as "Gloria's Girls." They were responsible for inserting electronic components into circuit boards, welds and quality control. Ken Olsen was known to drop in for coffee and a chat with Gloria to keep abreast of any production problems.

Why women on the production floor? Because it was no longer legal to hire children. Back in the woolen mill years, children were hired for their manual dexterity. In time, women had taken over those jobs. A DEC job opening advertisement from 1959 specified a preference for women with good eyesight and nimble fingers. Some women worked the "Mother Shift," meaning their day ended in time for them to be home when their kids got out of school.

Women working in the assembly area at Building 12, circa 1960. *Courtesy of Digital Equipment Corporation.*

Digital was not averse to hiring women with technical expertise, but some of the customers had a hard time adapting. Olsen had gone to the MIT campus to interview students in the electrical engineering department in 1960. One result was the hiring of Barbara Stephenson in 1961. Barbara recalled:

> *I was the first woman engineer at DEC. Customers would call for an applications engineer. They would say, "I want to speak with an engineer," and I would reply, "I'm an engineer," and they would say, "No, I want to speak with a real engineer." I developed this patter: "Well, tell me about the application you have in mind. We have three lines of modules ranging from five to ten megacycles and..." The line would go dead for a moment and then I'd hear, "Hey Joe, guess what, I've got a...woman...engineer on the phone!"*

Women were promoted from within. Rose Ann Giordano was hired from Xerox in 1979 to work in marketing, promoted to manager in 1981 and then promoted in 1984 to become the first woman vice-president. Earlier, Maynard resident Angela Cossette was hired as an administrative assistant in 1963 in support for DEC Users' Society. DECUS provided a pre-Internet forum for computer users to exchange technical information and user-developed software. Cossette moved up to becoming the company's first woman manager, in time with as many as one hundred people reporting to her. She recalled, "Digital became very aggressive about giving women the opportunity to grow in their careers and making it possible for them to move into key positions."

Cossette's comment reflected Digital's self-realization that it had a potential problem of being a white male–dominated technology company. An effort to counter this moved into higher gear with the hiring of African American John Sims as manager of affirmative action and equal employment opportunity in 1974. He rose to become vice-president of corporate personnel in 1984. Early on, the "Efficacy" program was available to help hundreds of employees to deal with uncertainty, take responsibility for their careers and manage their own career development. In addition, in a 1986 interview for *Black Engineer*, Sims explained, "Very early on we recognized that there were not enough minorities and women flowing into technical careers." The company started programs in scores of high schools and junior colleges with equipment gifts and funding. The company also deliberately located manufacturing plants in Black and Hispanic neighborhoods and trained staff there to qualify for promotion to management.

Barbara Walker, an African American lawyer with years of experience as director in the Office of Civil Rights in the federal government, joined DEC in 1979. She started "Core Groups," as monthly meetings at the senior management level, later expanded downward across the company, with the premise that "affirmative action is for everyone." Walker's training program began with self-assessment of one's own stereotypes. Workshop participants were expected to build relationships with people they felt were different from them. People were expected to talk about how they felt victimized by those perceptions. These groups of seven to nine people met on company time several hours per month to discuss the different expectations of people who were racial minorities, were women, were people from different countries or had different religious beliefs or were people with non-heterosexual orientations. The "Valuing Differences" program, which evolved from the core groups in the early 1980s, called for employees to acknowledge differences among their co-workers rather than pretending they did not exist. The stated goal was for the company and its employees to pay attention to differences of individuals and groups, to be comfortable with those differences and to utilize those differences as assets to the company's productivity.

Digital was ahead of its time with this work. The company had a zero-tolerance, non-discrimination policy toward gays and provided for internal gay support groups. This was in addition to the diversity and differences groups. Support groups were also encouraged for women. Managers who violated anti-discrimination policies were terminated. Were benefits quantifiable? DEC gained a reputation as a good workplace for minorities and women. The company attracted top talent, and staff turnover was below national norms. All employees felt empowered to identify problems and propose solutions. This fit well with a DEC mantra, "He who proposes, does," meaning that a person identifying a problem was often charged with putting together a team to fix it.

DIGITAL CREDIT UNION, DECWORLD AND HELICOPTERS

DCU

The Digital Federal Credit Union, which goes by DCU, had its beginnings in 1979, when DEC was in the process of transferring people from Maynard to a new factory in Westminster, thirty miles west on Route 2. Complaints got back to Ken Olsen that people were having a hard time getting house mortgages. After discussions with Human Resources, a decision was made to create a credit union that would charge less than the going rate for home loans and pay better interest on savings. Interestingly, this echoed services that the woolen mill had offered under the Maynard family during the nineteenth century. Back then, there was no bank in Maynard, so employees could earn interest by creating accounts funded by money deducted from their pay.

DCU has outlived Digital by more than twenty years. The headquarters are in Marlborough. It is the largest credit union headquartered in New England, with more than 863,000 members and management of assets in excess of $8 billion. Per DCU's website, "The credit union is a member-owned financial cooperative providing financial banking services to multiple member groups, but primarily serves communications and utilities employees. Membership is also open to immediate family of current members."

The DCU vision, "All Members Achieve Their Financial Goals Collaboratively," means that it wants to be catalyst and cheerleader for members' long-term financial success. DCU feels strongly that integrity is the most important aspect of what it is, so it stands by three principles that guide the decisions and behavior of everyone at DCU: 1) People Come First, 2) Do the Right Thing and 3) Make a Difference. The second, especially, harkens back to a guiding principle that stood Digital Equipment Corporation in good stead for so many years. In October 2004, the Digital Federal Credit Union and the City of Worcester entered into a naming rights partnership at $5.2 million for ten years to rename the arena and convention center to the DCU Center Arena & Convention Center. Naming rights were later extended to 2025.

DECworld

When Digital Equipment Corporation ruled the computer world, it was epitomized by the one-company trade show known as DECworld (or DEC

This poster for DECworld '87, acknowledging the last-minute need to charter two ships for convention attendee housing. *Courtesy of Maynard Historical Society.*

World). In 1987, the event brought forty-two thousand people to Boston. Just weeks before the September opening day, senior management realized that it had underestimated the housing demand and that all hotels in Boston were 100 percent booked. The solution? Jack Shields, marketing senior vice-president, proposed chartering ships. DEC contracted to have the *Queen Mary II* and the *Starship Oceanic*, also known as the "Big Red Boat," docked at Boston for the duration of the convention. The event cost DEC an estimated $20 million but generated close to $1 billion in product orders and service contracts.

DECworld had started as DEC Town in 1982 as an annual convention for employees—primarily for the sales force to be made familiar with the year's innovations and new product introductions. According to an anecdote from employee Jack Conaway, Ken Olsen showed up at the Digital exhibit at a CAD/CAM Expo on the West Coast and immersed himself in talking to DEC's booth staff and the customers. A while later, Ken's office announced DEC Town, the precursor for the highly successful DECworld, that extended this model to all the applications and industries that Digital served. DECworld 1988 was held in Cannes, France. Two years later, the company split up the event: DECworld in July was in Boston, followed by DECville in Cannes in September. DECworld 1992 was the last ever of these conventions.

Helicopters and Airplanes

Although never actually called "DEC Air," Digital had a fleet of helicopters that regularly flew routes to nearby facilities in New Hampshire, as well as to Boston's Logan International Airport. The landing pad in Maynard was at the rear of the fifty-five-acre complex on Parker Street (now "Maynard Crossing"). From Jack Falvey's book *Hot Negative*: "The helicopters were not executive perks at DEC; they were used by any and all employees who wanted to avoid traffic in going from place to place. This egalitarian policy further emphasized just how different DEC was and how indifferent they appeared to be to the cost of anything. In doing the case study, we were told that DEC had state-of-the-art video-conferencing facilities that no one used because it was sexier to take the helicopters."

Paul V. McGovern, an ex-marine and Vietnam veteran, was Digital's first helicopter pilot. Most of the pilots were veterans. One frequent user of the helicopters described how she lived in Wayland and had offices in both

Marlborough, Massachusetts, and Merrimack, New Hampshire. She could drive to the Parker Street complex, park, get on the scheduled helicopter and be in Merrimack about twenty minutes later. There, DEC had built a brand-new 1-million-square-foot facility and, out back, constructed a little log cabin with a potbellied stove and a location sign on it as if it were a railroad station to act as a place to keep warm while waiting for the flights to Massachusetts.

Freight jets flew regular schedules from Hanscom Field, Bedford, to DEC factories in Puerto Rico, Ireland and other locations. Part of the cargo hold near the front had a few rows of seats bolted to the floor, as well as access to the crew's toilet. Employees on company business could reserve seats on a first-come, first-serve basis. This was not senior management flying on luxury corporate jets.

In addition to the hired air force, Ken Olsen was himself a certified pilot. He owned his own plane and at times flew himself to "Woods Meetings" (senior management retreats) in Maine and New Hampshire—a thought that surely worried the rest of senior management at Digital! The solution was not to ask him to stop flying, but rather to insist that he have a professional as a copilot.

Chapter 9

1971–2021

Third Fifty Years

Maynard's centennial saw a thriving town of almost ten thousand people, once again dominated by a single company: Digital Equipment Corporation. Over the next fifty years, growth stalled as the town weathered two boom-to-bust cycles at the mill: the demise of Digital, followed by the rise and fall of Clock Tower Place. New schools and outdoor recreation were parts of Maynard's transformation.

BUSINESSES MORE THAN FIFTY YEARS OLD

A handful of Maynard businesses present at the centennial made it to the sesquicentennial, the criteria being that they started here and had no name changes. For some, the founding family is still involved. Gruber Bros. Furniture gets honorary mention, even though the doors closed in 2015.

Fowler-Kennedy Funeral Home

This establishment celebrated its 150th anniversary the same year as the town of Maynard! Henry Fowler, a signer of the 1871 petition to create the town of Maynard, was an undertaker. His son, Orrin S. Fowler, followed into the family business in 1887. Orrin's son, Guyer Fowler, moved the business to the

Concord Street location in 1941. There he continued the family trade until a year before his death, selling the business to John A. Kennedy in 1955. The business was renamed Fowler-Kennedy. Kennedy sold the business to John E. Erb, his son-in-law, in 1981. The business was, in turn, sold to Glenn D. Burlamachi in 2014 and to Matthew M. Farrow in 2017. Thus, we have a business without a current connection to the owners that gave it a name, but the occupation remains the same.

Parker Hardware

Thomas F. Parker opened the store in the Amory Block building (later Gruber Bros. Furniture). Parker moved to Nason Street, back to Main and then to its present location at 239 Main in 1980. An envelope in the historic society collection reads, "Since 1892, Your Friendly Store," providing "Hardware, Paint, Oils, Etc." The present-day owners—no relation to Parker—have been running the business since 1970.

Gruber Brothers Furniture

The original building, three stories tall, was known as the Amory Block and dated to 1868. A meeting hall on the second floor served as host to Maynard's first town meeting on April 27, 1871. Julius and Benjamin Gruber bought the building in 1919. Upstairs was Riverside Theatre (motion pictures), managed by Samuel Lerer. After a 1934 fire, the structure was rebuilt into a one-story building with Gruber Bros. Furniture as its sole occupant. Burton "Burt" Gruber, Julius's son, inherited the business. In a 1982 interview, he had recounted a story about selling sixty-nine dollars' worth of office furniture on credit to a few guys starting a business named Digital Equipment Corporation. When Burt retired, operation of the business went to his nephew, Joel B. Cohen.

Gruber closed its doors in November 2015—three generations and ninety-eight years as a family business. As Joel put it, "When I was sixteen years old, my mother sent me over to the store to help with a furniture delivery. Now, fifty-four years and one hip replacement later, it's time for me to get off the truck and retire." As of 2020, the building is slated for destruction to make way for a four-story brick apartment building with retail tenants on the first floor.

Although dating to 1868, the Gruber Bros. Furniture building had been through so many renovations that there was nothing left to be considered for historic preservation.

Maynard Country Club

Golf got off to an irregular start in 1916 with a few three-hole courses. This engendered enough excitement that when the sixty-eight-acre Calvin Whitney farm was put on the market in the summer of 1921, it was purchased with the intent to create a nine-hole golf course. By mid-September, sixty men were laboring on the nascent course, two hundred from Maynard and neighboring towns had joined the club and six holes were ready to play! The formal opening was the following July. Women were allowed to play if their husbands were members. Flash-forward ninety years and the country club was in decline. The town opted to buy the golf course in the fall of 2012 for $2 million versus letting it go to residential development. Approaching its centennial year, the golf course remains a golf course, with the clubhouse having become the Maynard Senior Center for the Council on Aging.

Hawes Florist

The Hawes family was operating out of Sudbury, using greenhouses. In 1932, Hawes opened a florist's shop on Nason Street. Victor Tomly worked there part time while in school, and then in 1961, he and his wife, Marion, bought the business, as the next generation of Hawes family members were not interested. The Tomlys moved the business to 70 Powder Mill Road in 1971. Victor's daughter, Melissa, is carrying on the family tradition.

Butler Lumber

Doing business since 1938 and currently going by Butler Lumber, Pipe and Stone, the company has been at 67 Parker Street since 1947. The name comes not from being family-owned, but rather because it got started on Butler Avenue. Ron and Helga Starr owned it from 1973 to 2019. Mike Sawvelle then made the transition from longtime manger to owner. Butler offers construction supplies of all sorts, plus a wide assortment of tools. The operating philosophy appears to be that if everything possible is in stock, nothing will ever have to be special ordered.

Erikson's Ice Cream

Hans Eriksen starting a dairy farm and milk delivery business in Stow along White Pond Road in 1902. Home delivery was by horse and wagon. His son, Hans Eriksen Jr., returned from serving in the U.S. Army in France during World War I and took up the family business, which by this time had shifted to buying milk from local farmers rather than milking their own cows. Hans Eriksen Jr. moved the dairy to its present site, just inside Maynard's border, in 1937 and started the ice cream business. The family name and business name were changed to Erikson after World War II.

The fourth generation now manages the business, and their children have put in time scooping ice cream. Over the years, Erikson's has provided summer employment to hundreds of high school students. Many of the alumni make a point of stopping in at Erikson's when visiting family or old friends still living in the area.

A "Green Monster" ice cream cone at Erikson's Ice Cream. The name is in reference to the famous green-painted wall at Fenway Park, home to the Boston Red Sox.

Pleasant Café

This is Maynard's oldest food/drink establishment, with its website noting, "Serving cold beer since 1945." According to a walking tour compiled by the Maynard Historical Commission, the building was constructed around 1899. Earlier tenants were the Cleary & Williams Dry Goods and Millinery, Jersey Butter Company, Arena & Sons Grocery and the Royal Café. The Pleasant Café, also known as the "PC," actually dates farther back than 1945. The town's 1936 business directory lists an establishment by that name at a different address. The current owners confirm that the family business opened at 157½ Main Street around 1934–35, closed for World War II and then reopened at the current site after the war.

Fine Arts Theatre

Although the Coughlans (father James and son Burton) were both involved with Peoples' Theatre, Burton decided to build his own theater on the family property at 17 and 19 Summer Street. James had started there with a horse stable in 1897, later adding an auto repair shop. Burton's vision, the luxuriously appointed Fine Arts Theatre, with four hundred seats, opened on June 29, 1949, with a showing of *The Red Shoes*. An adjoining second theater (later split in two) was added in 1969. The theater remained a Coughlan-owned property (under Burton's daughter) until it was sold in 2013. Steven Trumble has been the owner since then, carrying on what the Coughlans had started years earlier.

John's Cleaners

The oldest mention of this business is as a sponsor of the Maynard High School yearbook *Screech Owl* for 1963. The business may be a few years older than that. It was started by the son of the owner of the Maynard Coal Company, which had operated out of the other side of the building until 1965.

The Paper Store

Bob Anderson began this business in Maynard in 1964 as newspaper and magazine shop. Over time, his wife, sons and daughters joined the business. Still family-owned, the business has expanded to more than eighty stores across New England and into the mid-Atlantic states. Intriguingly, the name appears to be far older than the business. Starting in 1908, James "Jim" Ledgard had a store at that site that was informally known as "the paper store," as it sold newspapers and magazines. The store on Nason Street was closed in 2020, with intention to open in a brand-new building at the Parker Street complex.

Ray & Sons Cyclery

This business has served the bicycle trade since 1969. Prior to that, it was Ray's TV—same site, same family. In the early 1950s, it was Millstream Café—different family, different business. The restaurant was on the main floor, with the barroom downstairs. This explains the fancy wood floor.

The faded sign of Ray & Sons Cyclery indicates when the family business changed from televisions to bicycles.

Jarmo's Auto Repair

Located east of the east end of Main Street, Jarmo's is a full-service automotive repair center. The business was started by R. Michael "Jarmo" Jarmulowicz III in Concord and moved to Maynard in 1969. Previously, the site had been Barber Chevrolet. The building itself dates to 1920, when it was erected by William Holly and John and Herbert Comeau for their moving company. Earlier still, the site had been Maynard's two-classroom high school (1877–92).

Maynard Outdoor Store

Under this name, it just barely makes fifty years. An Army & Navy Surplus store opened in Maynard in 1950 just south of the Peoples' Theatre building. It moved to 24 Nason Street in 1968 and shortly thereafter changed its name to the Maynard Outdoor Store. At the same site, from 1942 to 1967, it had been home to an A&P supermarket. The façade of the Outdoor Store features a panel that reads "Case Bld 28," referring to W.B. Case & Sons, dry goods (clothing, shoes, hats, gloves and so on), with the building built in 1892. Case went out of business around 1935.

EVOLUTION OF A SCHOOL SYSTEM

Surprisingly, the two oldest school buildings—predating the creation of Maynard—are still with us. In the spelling of the era, the goals were to "teach children to rede and wright and cast accounts." Sudbury appears to have voted in 1779 to build a one-room schoolhouse for the northwest district; in 1871, it was moved farther north to what is now the intersection of Routes 27 and 117, where it served as Maynard's "Turnpike School" until 1881. No longer a school, it moved again in 1884 to the corner of Concord and Acton Streets—a distance of one mile—where it abides as a private home. On the Stow side of the Assabet River, District No. 5 had a school constructed in 1766: the "Brick School." This was on Summer Street, hence it became a Maynard school in 1871. It was closed the following year, auctioned for a sale price of $105 and remained in place as part of the home at 101 Summer Street. Two other schools also predated Maynard. One two-room building at the site of present-day town hall served until the town decided to replace it with its first multiroom brick school at the same site. The other, the first school on Nason Street, was lower grades, then the first high school and then lower grades again.

School	**Years**	**Fate**
Brick School (Stow)	1766–1872	Exists
Turnpike School (Sudbury)	1800–1881	Exists
Main Street	1857–92; 1894–1902	Moved
Nason Street (HS#1)	1864–91 (HS 1871–77)	Fire/Moved
Acton Street (HS#2)	1877–92	Moved
Sudbury Street (Garfield)	1881–92	Condos
Nason Street (HS#3)	1892–1916	Fire (total loss)

Main Street (Wilson)	1903–42; 1948–52	Fire (total loss)
Bancroft (Coolidge)	1906–81	Empty
Summer Street (HS#4)	1916–64	artspace
Nason Street (Roosevelt)	1918–88	Library
Summer Street (JHS#1)	1926–2000	artspace
MHS (HS#5)	1964–2013	Fire/Demolished
Summer Street (Fowler)	1965–2000	Fire/artspace
MHS (HS#6)	2013–present	Current
Green Meadow	1956; 1988–present	Current
Fowler (JHS#2)	2000–present	Current

At the time of the incorporation of Maynard in 1871, the new town was served by ten teachers working in four small school buildings. Salaries were in the range of nine to fifteen dollars per week. The high school was a two-room wooden building on Nason Street. Enrollment was thirty-five students. Six years later, the high school classes relocated to a new two-room school on Acton Street, across from the east end of Main Street, leaving the Nason building to revert to elementary school.

The year 1892 saw a consolidation of Main, Nason, Acton and Sudbury schools into a two-story, twelve-room wooden building at the Nason Street site, on the same stone foundation that is now the first floor of the Maynard Public Library. For a time, this was Maynard's only school building, serving all grades. The high school graduating class of 1892 chose orange and black as the school colors. Mr. E. Elmer Galger, principal and acting superintendent, was paid a salary of $1,061.40 per year. At that time, state law required that a child shall go to school twenty weeks in each year until fourteen years old (changed to sixteen years old in 1913). It was not until 1898 that state law prohibited children under fourteen year of age from doing factory work.

Big changes to Maynard affected the school system. The mill went bankrupt in 1898 and then was purchased and reopened in 1899 by the American Woolen Company. Expansion added the very large Building 5 on the south side of the millpond in 1902. The workforce grew, as did the town's population: from 3,142 in 1900 to 6,390 in 1910. The population explosion of school-age children, especially in the Presidential Village housing development of 1901–3, led to the construction of new brick schools at the Main Street site (1903) and on Bancroft Street (1906). The first was

Bancroft/Coolidge School was an elementary school for seventy-five years. The original cost in 1906 was $20,831 ($600,000 in 2020 dollars) and then $12,000 to add a second floor in 1909. After its use as a school ended in 1981, the school system used the building for various purpose through 2014.

renamed Woodrow Wilson School in 1932. The second had a second floor of four more classrooms added in 1910 and was renamed Calvin Coolidge School in 1932.

On September 20, 1916, a nighttime fire brought an end to the Nason Street School. This was attributed to arson, as there had been a less damaging fire at the school just a week earlier. All that was left standing were the two brick chimneys. For a disaster, the timing was good. Three years earlier, the town had voted to build a new high school, with the site on Summer Street chosen later. The two-story brick building—currently the east wing of ArtSpace—was built at a cost of $61,500 and occupied on October 2, 1916. This was the high school through 1964. A new brick elementary school was constructed at Nason Street, atop the foundation of the fire site. It opened in the fall of 1918 and named Roosevelt School in 1919. It served as a school through 1988, stood empty almost twenty years and was resurrected as the Maynard Public Library in July 2006.

Meanwhile, back on Summer Street, the Town of Maynard, in its wisdom, decide to redirect a stream that flowed next to the high school into an underground storm sewer and build a junior high school, auditorium and gymnasium atop it (which is why Artspace is prone to flooding). The junior high opened in January 1926 and was named Emerson Junior High School in 1932. After the high school moved to its new south-side campus in 1964, half the building became Fowler Elementary School and the whole complex became known as Emerson-Fowler School. In time, the junior high school took over the entire building as Fowler Middle School, remaining as such until the end of 2000.

Meanwhile, back on Main Street, Wilson School was closed in 1942 because the school population had decreased dramatically; it was reopened in 1948, when the postwar baby boom started to arrive, and then was destroyed when a predawn fire on December 17, 1952, left only the scorched brick exterior standing. This left Coolidge and Roosevelt as elementary schools.

The next phase for the Maynard school system was to create three schools adjacent to one another on the south side of Route 117, with each to have adequate parking and adjacent fields for physical education classes. Green Meadow School was first. Land was taken from Crowe Park. The school opened in time for the 1956–57 school year. Coolidge was kept on until

The Woodrow Wilson school, located where the Maynard Town Building is now, existed for forty-nine years before being destroyed by fire in 1952. *Courtesy of Maynard Historical Society.*

1981. A major addition to Green Meadow approved in 1986, completed for the beginning of the 1988–89 year, led to the closing of Roosevelt in 1988. "Maynard High School" was completed in 1964 at a cost of $1.7 million. Fowler Middle School (leave the old building, keep the name) opened in 2000. And then, in 2013, the fifth Maynard High School was replaced by the sixth Maynard High School, at a cost of $42.5 million.

Note that over the years, two schools were completely destroyed by fire (Nason in 1916 and Wilson in 1952), and three were significantly damaged (Nason in 1879, the high school in 1992 and Emerson-Fowler in 1978).

Entering its 150th year, Maynard has two public schools under twenty-five years old and part of one (Green Meadow) approaching seventy-five years. The student population, which had peaked in the baby boom years at 2,106 students in 1971, has long since declined back to the mid-teens. WAVM (FM 91.7) had its first broadcast on April 22, 1974. Near fifty years later, about one hundred students from MHS and Fowler are active at WAVM and its cable TV and YouTube channels.

In 1965, St. Bridget's Parish opened St. Bridget's Parochial School in a brick building on Percival Street, in a filled-in section of the millpond. The school was staffed by the Sisters of Notre Dame, who had a modest convent nearby. The parochial school closed in 1986. Starting in 1995, the building became home to the Imago School, a private school offering a Christian faith-based education for grades from prekindergarten through eighth grade.

PARKS, TRAILS AND HISTORIC WALKING TOURS

Parks

Maynard is parsimonious about naming parks after people. Most residents are aware of Memorial Park (1925), at the corner of Summer and Nason Streets, as the site of Maynard's war memorials and also summer band concerts. The other named parks are John A. Crowe Park, Alumni Field, Carbone Park, John J. Tobin Waterfront Park, Reo Road Tot Lot, Coolidge Park, Maplebrook Park and Ice House Landing.

Reverend Crowe, pastor of St. Bridget's Church from 1894 to 1905, was instrumental in getting the town to buy the six acres and was also the first superintendent of the park. The park was named after him in 1908, but it took until 1915 for a metal plaque to be affixed to a standing stone reading

The land that became Crowe Park was purchased by the town in 1901. It was partially repurposed in 1954 to be the site of Green Meadow School. In the 1920s, it was on the circus circuit (with elephants!), and the 1960s saw annual carnivals. *Carnival photograph by Oliver (Swat) Warila, courtesy of Maynard Historical Society.*

"JOHN A. CROWE PARK, PURCHASED BY THE TOWN 1901." For years, the park sported a grandstand seating five hundred, and in 1939 it gained a fieldstone bandstand, courtesy of Depression-era federal projects. The bandstand was the summer site of Maynard Community Band concerts for decades, until it was torn down in the 1990s as unsafe. The park was host to baseball, football, soccer, cricket, track and field and other sports.

Next up is Alumni Field (1928), which has also been through a series of changes. From 1892 to 1947, the William Smith House on Great Road was owned by the town and used as the town poor farm. In 1928, part of this land was transferred to the school department. Football games started that fall; the site was later augmented by bleachers, a cinder track for running events, tennis courts, a hockey rink and a fieldhouse. Many of these improvements were Depression-era public works projects.

Land at the corner of Summer and Florida Streets was cleared for use as a park in 1972; it was named Carbone Park in 1987 to honor Walter Carbone, past member of the town's planning board and Conservation

Commission. A sign to this effect was erected circa 2005. This park is not much more than a grassy space with a few benches, backed by wooded wetlands with a rough trail, but every public green space is welcome in the densely developed core of this town.

John J. Tobin Riverfront Park (1989) occupies the compact space on either side of the footbridge over the Assabet River. Mr. Tobin had been a board of public works member for more than thirty years and also active at times on the town's Finance Committee, School Building Committee and the board of appeals. Tobin was instrumental in starting the Boys & Girls Club. He was so active in town that many people referred to him as "Mr. Maynard." Prior to the park's construction, the area had been a brownfield eyesore. Long after the trains had stopped running, the deteriorating trestle bridge (removed in 1980) and bordering land were overgrown, neglected and had become a hangout for town drunks, derelicts and the homeless. Men slept in corrugated cardboard shanties. The 2018 completion of the Assabet River Rail Trail, including a new bridge, brings many more people to this pocket park. This is one of the few places in town where it is possible to stand at the river's edge.

Ice House Landing (2002) is another access point to the Assabet River—in this case upstream of the Ben Smith Dam—providing access to the water for kayakers, canoeists and paddle boarders. A small parking lot at the end of Winter Street is convenient to the park and to the Rail Trail. During the warmer months, the town provides a kayak and canoe launch dock that doubles as a fishing dock, or just a place to sit and admire the river. The entrance is flanked by standing stones, one with a Thoreau quote: "River towns are winged towns."

The park's name refers to the older presence of an icehouse just to the east, where ice cut from the river on one side was shipped out via the railway on the other side. Remnants of the foundation of a building are seen a short distance from the park. The first icehouse on this site, built by J.R. Bent, burned in 1918, a fate common to many such establishments, as the basic design involved wooden double walls, with the spaces between filled with sawdust for insulation. A replacement, under a different owner, burned in 1922. A second replacement, again with a different owner, burned in 1950. Icehouses were often used as practice sites for basketball teams, as they would be empty of ice from late fall into early winter. Upside: wooden floors, high ceilings and lights. Downside: no heat.

Maplebrook Park, maintained by Maynard Community Gardeners since 1995, is at the intersection of Summer, Maple and Brook Streets. In 2017,

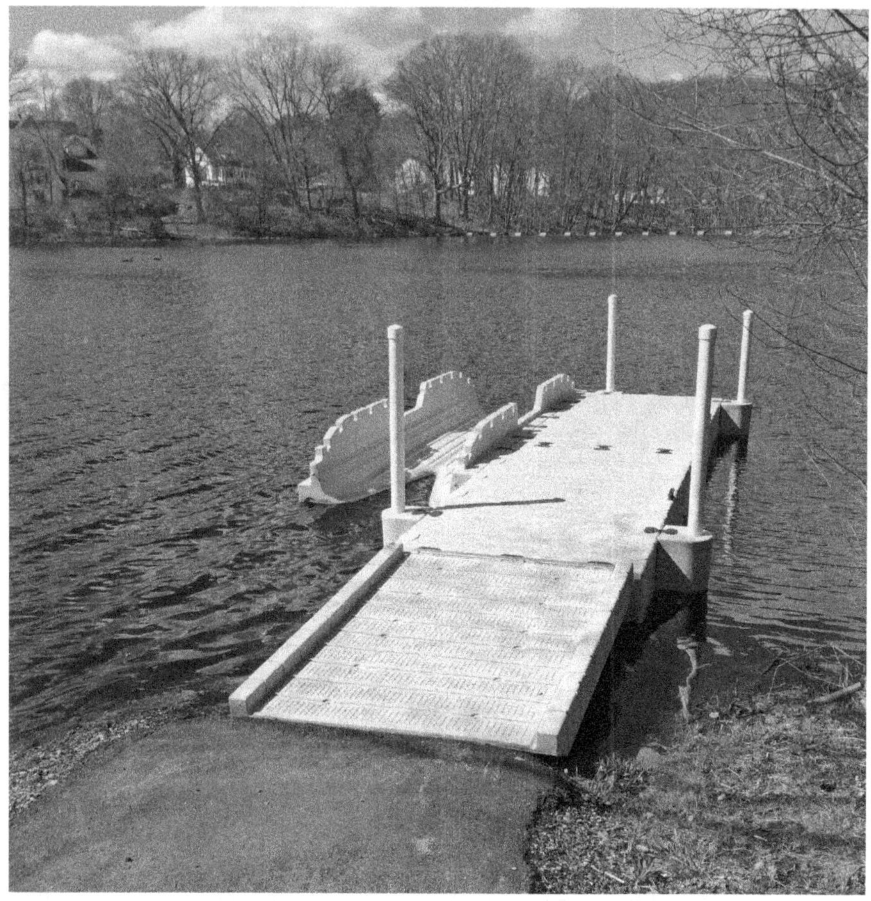

The Ice House Landing launch dock allows for people to launch and land without getting their feet wet. The orange floats in the distance warn people to keep a safe distance from the Ben Smith Dam.

the back third was lost to the creation of the Assabet River Rail Trail, but what remains is well maintained as a little greenspace oasis. Land for the Reo Road Tot Lot was purchased in 1969; the park was constructed in 1994 and renovated in 2014. Old but new again is Coolidge Park, dedicated in 2014. This greenspace had its origins as a playground for the Bancroft Street School, opened as a one-story brick building in 1906 and enlarged to a two-story building in 1911. Bancroft was renamed Calvin Coolidge School in 1932, closed in 1981 and then renovated in 1984 to become the home of the Maynard Public Schools Administration. The building was vacated in 2014. Throughout all these decades as a school and after, the hill and level area between the building and Route 27 found use as a sledding hill in winter and a playground in all seasons. In 2014, this officially became Coolidge Park Playground, with a hill slide, playground equipment, winter sledding and a T-ball field. The park will exist regardless of what happens to the building.

"No-Name Parks" can be applied to several greenspaces around town. A plan to build a town building and adjoining space for Maynard's library, later the police station, was approved in 1960 and dedicated on July 29, 1962. What was intended for the greenspace between the building and the river is a mystery. The Maynard Historic Society collection has an informal note in a "Parks" folder that reads in its entirely, "5/12/88: The little park in the rear of Maynard Bld has been grassed down, and when the fountain is set in motion it will make a refreshing spot to gaze upon." There is no fountain.

"No Name" also applies to a small plot of land behind the Holy Annunciation Orthodox Church, accessed from Lewis Street; informally, it is "Walcott Woods." Volunteers have at times joined forces to tame this part-grass, part-woods, part-wetlands pocket property into something park-like, but nature tends to win the battle. Likewise, the greenspace at the Marble Farm historic site, adjacent to the northern end of the Assabet River Rail Trail, is a volunteer-effort pocket park, abetted by the Trail of Flowers program planting thousands of daffodils there.

Other unnamed recreational spaces have vanished. Children no longer splash in the river behind town hall or skinny-dip at Bent Ice House. Ice skating took place on the millpond, Durant Pond, Thanksgiving Pond, Vose Pond and at "Cemetery Pond," a Depression-era project created in 1936. Located in its glory between Glenwood Cemetery and Route 117, it was a roughly triangular pond with a pathway around the border, an island in the middle and a small pond in the middle of the island. The pond has since reverted to a swamp.

Trails

On the town website, the Maynard Conservation Commission provides several maps of public open space and trails (townofmaynard-ma.gov/resources/trails). The maps cover Maynard's public open spaces and trails and provide a connection to maps for the Assabet River National Wildlife Refuge. Some of the town trails have signs at the trailheads and marks painted on trees and are maintained by an informal group of volunteers for usage by hikers and experienced off-road bicyclists. Volunteers also combat invasive plant species such as Oriental bittersweet, burning bush and multiflora rose. In town, School Woods, Summer Hill, Assabet River Walk and Rockland Avenue/Durant Pond offer interesting experiences. Wildlife sightings can include deer and turkeys. The Assabet River National Wildlife Refuge on the south side of town offers fifteen miles of trails, with some open to bicycling but none open to dogs. None of this is "virgin" land. Rather, all of it is past farm and pasture, gone to forest. Remnants of stone walls are testimony to colonial-era use.

Historic Walking Tours

Six printed tour guides have been produced by the Maynard Historical Commission and made available through a generous grant from the Maynard Cultural Council. Copies are available at town hall and the library (as well as online at townofmaynard-ma.gov). These tours provide a great way to learn about the history of our town:

- Main Street and the Mill
- Assabet Village
- New Village and Maynard's Hill
- Great Road
- Assabet River National Wildlife Refuge
- Glenwood Cemetery

MONUMENTS AND MARKERS

As a town where few (or no) famous events have ever taken place and few notable people ever lived or worked, Maynard is bereft of significant monuments to its glorious history. A root cause is that the town did not exist until 1871, so there's no Revolutionary War or Civil War history.

There are the named watering troughs. In 1881, when Maynard had a population of 2,350 people and 180 horses, a committee was appointed to consider the matter of public watering troughs. The idea went nowhere until a town water system was constructed in 1889. Between 1891 and 1904, four watering troughs were donated to the town, each with the name of the donating person or family inscribed. These provided a basin for horses, a ground-level bowl for dogs and a drinking fountain for their human companions. All four exist to this day, although now as flower planters, and not all are at their original locations. Lorenzo Maynard, Amory's oldest son, contributed a trough that originally stood at the corner of Nason and Main. The inscription reads, "GIFT OF L.M. 1891." This was moved to Main and Walnut, where it remained until 1951; then it was kept in storage until 1969, when at the request of the Maynard Historical Society it was placed in front of the fire and police station (now only the fire station) in preparation for the town's centennial celebration.

Mrs. Asahel Balcom donated "BALCOM MEMORIAL" in 1892 to stand at the intersection of Routes 117 and 27. "RAFFERTY MEMORIAL," dated 1892 but installed in 1894, was placed at the intersection of Main and Sudbury Streets; it was shifted a small distance east in 2017 to accommodate the Assabet River Rail Trail. A trough owned by Warren A. Haynes was inscribed after his death "W.A. HAYNES 1904" and relocated to the Concord and Acton Streets intersection.

The Haynes water trough had initially been located at Concord and Tremont. The Haynes family were early and prominent residents of what became Maynard in 1871, with Warren being a signer of one of the petitions to create the town.

At the corner of Summer and Concord Streets, there is a plaque on a metal pole reading, "ANTHONY J. DZERKACZ SQUARE." There are seven other plaques scattered about Maynard honoring George Daley, Frank J. Demars, Frank G. King, Edward Miller, John R. Murray, Ralph I. Panton and Myles J. Tierney. A visit to Memorial Park reveals these eight men as having died in World War I while enrolled in military service. These were installed on November 11, 1923. In the downstairs meeting room of town hall, there are photos of these men plus the thirty-three who died in service during World War II, one during the Korean War, three for Vietnam and one in Afghanistan. Their names and others from those who served and survived these various wars are inscribed on the monuments of Memorial Park. Without naming any names, there is a modest plaque on the Main Street Bridge (1922) dedicated to the women and men of Maynard who offered their lives in the Civil War, Spanish-American War and the world wars.

Other than war, Maynard's monuments are an eclectic collection. A standing stone at Concord and Acton Streets mentions the line of march of the minutemen on April 19, 1775. A stone west of the end of Old Marlboro Road is inscribed "RICE TAVERN 1700–1815." This wooded spot was an important crossroads long before Maynard was Maynard. However, even in Henry David Thoreau's time, this was the "old" Marlboro Road, as a newer, less swampy road had been built a bit to the south. The tavern had become a farmhouse. In his famous essay "Walking," he wrote about the pleasure of walking on an abandoned road—because it no longer went anywhere, it became a road that, in one's imagination, went everywhere:

If with fancy unfurled
You leave your abode,
You may go round the world
By the Old Marlborough Road.

Back in the center of town, a water fountain on Main Street is inscribed "IN MEMORY OF LUKE S. BROOKS." Brooks was a resident of what was then Stow. He was a Stow minuteman at the battle in Concord on April 19, 1775. The water fountain was installed in 1911, paid for by descendants of the Brooks family. A water fountain at Memorial Park is inscribed "MAYNARD WOMAN'S CLUB 1977." The newest monument in town is a marker at Walnut and Main: "KEN OLSEN PLAZA," a nod to the

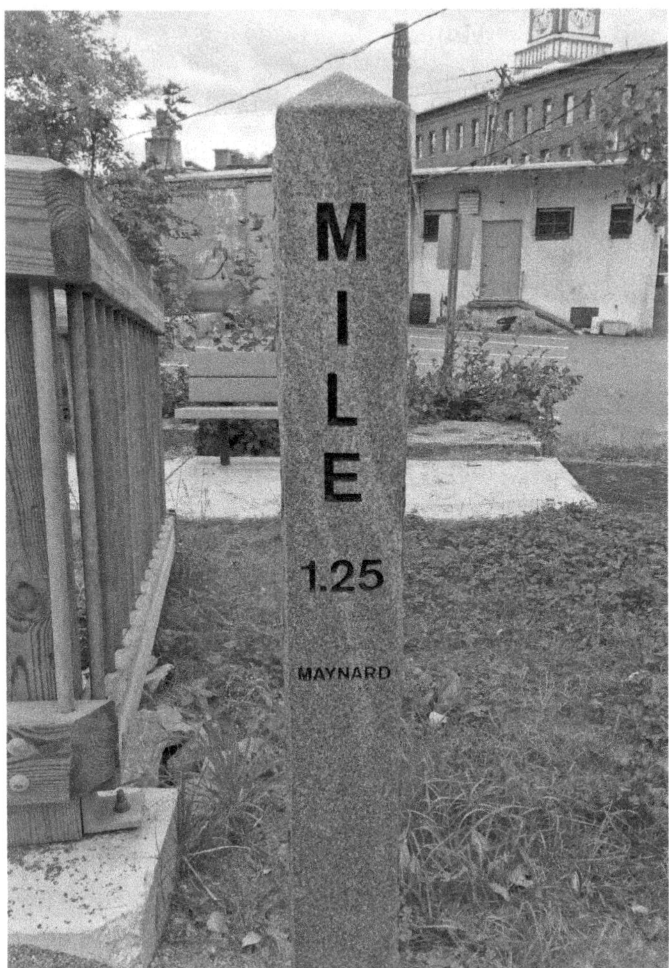

Granite posts mark every quarter mile on the Assabet River Rail Trail, starting with 0.0 at the Maynard/ Stow border. This one is in Tobin Park, next to the footbridge over the Assabet River.

years that Digital Equipment Corporation's international headquarters was the mill complex here in Maynard. Ken did not live here, but he and thousands of employees worked here. The clock tower itself can be considered a monument, as it was built by Lorenzo Maynard to honor his father, Amory, the cofounder of the woolen mill. The clock tower—showing the time as 12:10—has been featured on the town seal since January 1975.

Markers

Maynard has (or had) standing stone marking the borders of the town. The town is a five-sided polygon, with the border totaling 8.27 miles in length. Massachusetts State Act of 1871, Chapter 198, describes in detail how the lines were drawn. A 1904 atlas of the boundaries of the towns of Middlesex Country provided longitude and latitude for each of the five corners, a description of location relative to then current landmarks—some long since gone—and physical descriptions of stone markers erected at each corner. Recent visits confirmed that four of the five markers are exactly as described in the atlas. The southernmost stone was replaced by the U.S. Army in 1942 with a granite block embedded flush to the ground. The easternmost marker was knocked over in 2011 and has since been repaired.

The easiest marker to visit is on the Maynard/Sudbury line, adjacent to Route 27. A "S" on one side indicates Sudbury; a "M" on the other is for Maynard. The west-most stone is on private property, the north-most deep in town woods and the east-most stone is a puzzle. It stands at the touching point of Maynard, Acton, Concord and Sudbury, next to the entrance of the Concord Mews housing development. Hence, as one circles the stone, the order of letters should be M-A-C-S. The actual order is M-S-A-C.

The laws of the Commonwealth of Massachusetts (Title VII, Chapter 42, Section 2) require that each town is to have at least two of its selectmen or their designated substitutes visit each of its border markers every five years or so in order to confirm that the markers are still there. This is distinct from perambulating (walking) the entire boundary, the law for which has been repealed. These official visitors are to paint the year of their visit on their town's side of the marker. Maynard has been oft remiss but did mark the markers in 2011 and is expected to do so again for the sesquicentennial year.

There is also a set of much newer markers through the center of town. With the completion of the Maynard section of the Assabet River Rail Trail, there are granite posts every quarter of a mile, starting with 0.00 miles at the Stow/Maynard border and finishing with 2.25 miles just before the Maynard/Acton border. Once across, Acton markers start at 0.00 miles.

THE ASSABET RIVER NATIONAL WILDLIFE REFUGE

Origins of the refuge date back to the 1942 seizure of land spanning Maynard, Sudbury, Hudson and Stow via federal eminent domain. Landowners were given as little as ten days to pack up and leave. The site was chosen to be convenient for transportation of munitions to the Boston Navy Yard yet far enough inland so that German battleships could not shell the area. There was no risk of airplane bombing, as the German navy did not have any aircraft carriers.

The refuge—which includes one-fifth of Maynard's land area—covers 3.5 square miles of woodland, wetland, ponds and streams. Biological surveys have identified more than 650 plant species, 135 bird species, 25 mammal species, 17 reptile species and 19 fish species. The prime purpose is to manage land for migratory bird conservation.

A website maintained by Friends of the Assabet River National Wildlife Refuge has maps, photos, activities and a link to the government's refuge

Massachusetts is home to more than 100,000 whitetail deer. Eastern Massachusetts between Routes 128 and 495 has 15 to 30 per square mile. Statewide, hunting takes about 13,000 per year. Vehicle collisions kill an additional 8,000. Hunting is not allowed on Sundays.

website. There is a wonderfully informative, child-friendly visitor center at 680 Hudson Road, Sudbury. For people who just want to park and roam, the north parking lot is accessed from White Pond Road, reachable from Route 117 in Stow. Within the refuge there are fifteen miles of old roads and new walking trails, with the old roads (in poor repair) open to bicycles. No dogs or other pets are allowed anywhere in the refuge, as well as no horses, no fires, no overnight camping, no ATVs, no dirt bikes and no snowmobiles. One of the most interesting features of the refuge are the fifty World War II–era ammunition bunkers. Bunker no. 303 is sometimes open for tours.

Deer hunting is allowed in the refuge. This is an example of a need to manage a native species acting like an invasive species. Unrestricted hunting through the 1800s resulted in the New England extinction of wolves and mountain lions and the near extinction of whitetail deer. But with restrictions on hunting and a return of farmland to wilderness, the Massachusetts deer population is roughly 100,000 or 10 per square mile—and much higher in favorable terrain. Without population management of some sort, deer destroy ecological balance. ARNWR allows deer hunting so it will be a refuge for all wildlife—not just deer.

THE ASSABET RIVER RAIL TRAIL

People with long memories can recall the end of Maynard's railroad passenger service on May 16, 1958. Less noted was the end of freight service in the 1960s. After decades of disuse, the railroad gave up on resurrecting rail service. The 12.4-mile-long right of way was deeded over to the five communities (Acton, Maynard, Stow, Hudson and Marlborough). Some of the land was subsequently sold to private owners. And there it lay, a broken-up ghost of a railroad spur dating back to the 1850s, once traveled by as many as twenty trains a day, with crossties rotting and trees growing up between the rails.

The concept of converting obsolete railroads to pathways for non-motorized use (i.e., "rails-to-trails") began in Wisconsin in 1967. Important milestones included the National Trails System Act, which allowed for conversion of government-granted railroad right of ways be converted to trails, and the Transportation Equity Act, which permitted federal funding for transportation improvements other than in support of planes, trains and automobiles. Locally, the vision of a rail trail from Acton to Marlborough was established in 1992 by a few interested residents acting in concert with town employees This led to the creation of the Assabet River Rail Trail (ARRT) organization to coordinate volunteer activity. For Acton and Maynard, that included literally hundreds and hundreds of hours clearing and maintaining the right of way for hikers and bikers. While a few people have been ambivalent about the planned trail ("It's right behind my house!" or "Why does it have to be paved?"), most of the comments were positive. Jeff Richards was the first ARRT president, followed by Thomas Kelleher, who served in that position from 2001 onward. Duncan Power has been clerk for as long.

After many long years, federal and state funding was approved for the north end of the trail. A ceremony in Maynard on Thursday, July 21, 2016, celebrated groundbreaking for the $6.7 million construction of 3.4 miles of trail from the Acton Street station to the Maynard/Stow border. Town Managers Kevin Sweet (Maynard) and Roland Bartl (Acton) described how this project would make both towns friendlier to pedestrians and cyclists; both also noted that their towns participate in the state's Complete Streets program. The contractor for this multi-year project was D'Allessandro Corporation.

More than six hundred trees, some as much as a foot in diameter, were stuffed into a super-sized wood chipper. As partial compensation, the budget included more than $200,000 for landscaping, including the planting of

Drone photograph of the installation of the Rail Trail bridge over the Assabet River. *Courtesy of D'Allessandro Corporation.*

about one hundred trees. Old rails were sold for scrap. Centered in the resulting eighteen-foot-wide swath was a twelve-foot-wide, asphalt-paved trail. Among the changes in Maynard included the following: Ice House Landing, off Winter Street, got a paved parking lot, some parking was lost from the town lot and part of Maplebrook Park was sacrificed. The six-foot-wide wooden footbridge over the Assabet River was replaced by a wood-planked, steel truss bridge sixty-two feet long and sixteen feet wide. "Distance travelled" markers were installed every quarter-mile. Signage was created to describe historic sites adjacent to the trail. A ribbon-cutting ceremony took place on August 10, 2018. Massachusetts Department of Transportation (MassDOT) secretary Stephanie Pollack joined state and local officials at the event.

The south end of this portion of the trail terminates at an entrance to the Assabet River National Wildlife Refuge, which offers fifteen miles of trails, half open to bicycling. Trail walkers and cyclists are also permitted to continue two miles farther west on the unpaved, privately owned "Track Road," which ends at Sudbury Road, Stow. This project added trail miles to what had been built in 2006 in Hudson and Marlborough. Connecting the two ends along the route of the original railroad would cover 3.2 miles and cross the Assabet River twice.

YOU KNOW YOU'RE FROM MAYNARD IF...

You can remember forty or more of the following: 17 Summer Restaurant, 51 Main Street Restaurant, A&P supermarket, Alchemist Health Foods, Allen's Café, Alphonse's Powder Mill Restaurant, Amory's, Army & Navy Surplus Store, Assabet Institute for Savings, Assabet River Rail Trail (before it was paved), Avalon Restaurant, Bacharach's Grocery, Bank of America, Batley & Sons Florists, Battle Road, Bikeworx motorcycle shop, Boeske's gas station, Brick Oven Pizza...

Getting driving lessons from Bug-Eyed Bob, Café La Mattina, Carbone's Twin Tree Café, Cast Iron Kitchen, Center Dance Studio, Ciro's Restaurant, Clock Tower Place, the Clothes Inn, Colonial Theater (movies for nine cents), Congregational Church, Copper Kettle Restaurant, The Corner Closet consignment store, the Crowe Park bandstand, Dennison Manufacturing Company, working for Digital Equipment Corporation, Donutland, Easter egg hunts at Crowe Park, Elizabeth Schnair's newsstand, the Elmwood Street

Phil Bohunicky
As a young orphan boy, Phil learned the harsh realities of life. As an adult, he has dedicated his life to bringing joy and laughter to Maynard's children through his sponsoring of the annual Christmas Parade and his Fleepo the Clown shows.

Phil, in his alter ego Fleepo the Clown, was instrumental in starting the Maynard Christmas Parade tradition in 1966. Phil left us for the Big Circus in the Sky in 2004. *Courtesy of Maynard Historical Society.*

bathhouse and sauna, the Factory Outlet store, feeding millpond ducks and geese at the farmers' market…

The fire station horn sounding at 12:10 p.m., Fleepo the Clown (aka Philip Bohunicky), Flipside Records, the flood of August 1955 (Hurricane Diane), Fraternal Order of Eagles, Fred's TV, the Gail Shop, Geek Boutique, Gramps' Garage, Grandmothers' Trunk, Grappas Restaurant, Gruber Bros. Furniture, the gym at Emerson-Fowler School, Halfway Café, Happy Toe Square Dancers, the old high school (and the older old high school), the hurricane of 1938, ice skating on Cemetery Pond, Irene's Stitch-It Shop, JJ Newberry variety store, Jacob's Market, Jimmy's Variety, John J. Tobin ("Mr. Maynard"), Johnson Pharmacy…

Kelly's Bowling Lanes (candlepin, of course), Knights of Columbus building, Leapin' Lena appearing in parades, Lovell Bus Line, M&B Lunch, Main and Nason Streets' two-way traffic, Manning Pharmacy, Massa's Bakery, Martin & Doran Funeral Home, the Charles A. Welch Lodge in the Masonic Building, Maydale Beverage Company, Maynard's centennial celebration, peeking through the door into the Maynard family crypt, Maynard High School bonfires at homecoming, Maynard Motel, Maynard Smoke Shop…

The Methodist church, Monster.com, motorcycle charity rides parading through town and ending at the Rod and Gun Club, Mr. Takeout, Murphy & Snyder Printers, Nason Street Spa, New Idea Store, Northern Recording Studio, "Only in Maynard" T-shirts, Oriental Delight, Parker Street Hall (the Finnish Workingmen's Socialist Society), the two-level town parking garage (1984–2014), Patty's Donut Shop, Paul's Bakery…

Peoples' Theatre, Prescott Paint, Priest's Café, Quarterdeck Seafoods, Quinteros, the railroad station (passenger trains to Boston until 1958), the Red Door (and Ma), Rickles Cut Rate, River Rock Café, Rob Henry's Tavern, Rodoff Shalom Synagogue, Russo's restaurant, St. Casimir's Polish Catholic Church, St. George's Episcopal Church, St. John's Finnish Evangelical Lutheran Church, Salamone's, Samuels Studio, Santa arriving for the Christmas parade by helicopter, school trips to the clock tower to see the clock, *Screech Owl* yearbooks…

Sears & Roebucks catalogue store, Sheehan and White Funeral Home, shooting rats at the town dump, Sid's Airport, drinking Bud Light on Silver Hill, live music at the Sit N' Bull Tavern, skating at Thanksgiving Pond, sledding at the golf course, Sons of Italy, Speedy's Pizza, Stretch's Tavern,

Monster.com, at one time a famous technology disruptor in the jobs search industry, was a major presence at the mill from 1998 to the spring of 2014. Its departure hastened the end of Clock Tower Place.

Summer Street Fine Consign, T.C. Lando's Sub & Pizzeria, Taurus Leather Shop, Taylor Chevrolet, horrible smells from the Taylor mink ranch, Tennis Court Dances, Teresina's vintage clothing, Tobin's Pizza, Town Paint, Tutto's bowling alley and pool hall, United Co-op, Victory Market, Vincent's Antiques, W.A. Twombly Funeral Home, walking the trestle, W.B. Case & Sons, Western Auto, Willy Philly's sandwich shop, the Woodrow Wilson School fire (1952), going to a woodsy, Woolworth's and Ye Olde Town House Pub…

Please share this list with people who have moved away from Maynard. Who knows, maybe they will move back.

Chapter 10

2021–FUTURE

Next Fifty Years

What is history? Perhaps it's "Everything up until this morning's cup of coffee." Maynard's history is well served by books recounting how the land was acquired from Native Americans or what brought the various immigrant groups here, but some space needs to be dedicated to what is happening now—and next—lest it pass unrecorded and soon forgotten.

PRESERVING HISTORY

The Maynard Historical Society was started in June 1961. Per the founding documents, "The purpose of the organization is to gather all available historical data and facts to be used in preparation of the history of Maynard and to preserve and perpetuate these records, together with all historical objects and materials received by the society."

The nascent historical society gave birth on March 5, 1962, to the Maynard Historical Committee—formally established and funded by the Town of Maynard—to compile a history in anticipation of a centennial celebration planned for April 1971. The Committee began with five members: Albert Alexanian Jr., Mary Alexanian, Janette Taylor, Frank Lituri and James Farrell. Nine years later, with the comings and goings of several members in between, the centennial project was completed by a Committee consisting of Ralph Sheridan, Birger Koski, Elizabeth Schnair,

Winnifred Hearon and Eileen Kozak. The efforts of the Committee members and many other volunteers culminated with the publication of *A History of Maynard, 1871–1971*, sometimes referred to as "The Blue Book" due to the cover color. The press run was of 425 hardcover and 641 softcover copies. All were sold.

The Committee ended its existence concurrent with the celebration of the centennial, superseded by the Maynard Historical Commission, which exists to the present day. The Commission's mission as an official Town of Maynard entity is "To preserve, protect and develop the historic and archaeological assets of the community and ensure that the goals of historic preservation are considered in the planning and future development of the community."

One program of the MHC is to highlight historical business buildings and privately owned homes with plaques that document the year these buildings were constructed and original owners. Over the years, MHC successfully submitted proposals to the town for Community Preservation Act funding to restore the official town scale, on display on the second floor of the Maynard Public Library, and in 2015 to replace the Depression-era cast-iron fence at Glenwood Cemetery. This cemetery is the only site or structure in Maynard that is in the National Register of Historic Places (NR# 04000425). That status was achieved in May 2004.

In conjunction with the Maynard Cultural Council, self-guided history walking tour brochures were created by MHC member Peggy Jo Brown, available free at the library and town hall or downloadable at home. Meanwhile, the very nongovernment, very volunteer Maynard Historical Society focuses on scanning pictorial and print documents into secure archival storage and also cataloguing thousands of the documents in a searchable online database that can be found by searching for "Maynard Historical Society Archives." These preservation efforts are an ongoing project funded, in part, from a Community Preservation Act (CPA) grant from the Town of Maynard. In addition to print and photograph documents, the society has a wonderful collection of historical artifacts. For example, when the 1892 clock tower clocks were renovated by Digital Equipment Corporation in 1980, one set of the original clock hands made its way into the society's keeping.

For anyone interested in learning about the history of Maynard, these immensely useful books are available at the Maynard Library:

- *A Brief History of the Town of Maynard*, by William H. Gutteridge (1921)

Maynard is much younger than its "parent" towns of Sudbury (1639) and Stow (1683), yet a lot of history has been written—the book you are holding in your hand is the tenth about the history of Maynard. The town library has all these plus the town's annual reports.

- *A History of Maynard, 1871–1971*, Town of Maynard Historical Committee (1971)
- *Maynard Massachusetts*, Images of America, by Paul Boothroyd and Lewis Halpin (1999)
- *Assabet Mills*, Images of America, by Paul Boothroyd and Lewis Halpin (1999)
- *Maynard*, Postcard History Series, by Paul Boothroyd and Lewis Halpin (2005)
- *Hometown Soldiers: Civil War Veterans of Assabet Village and Maynard Massachusetts*, by Peggy Jo Brown (2005)
- *Maynard, Massachusetts: A House in the Village*, by Jan Voogd (2007)
- *Maynard: History and Life Outdoors*, by David A. Mark (2011)
- *Hidden History of Maynard*, by David A. Mark (2014)

In 2006, Maynard voters adopted a Community Preservation Act and then formed a Community Preservation Committee (CPC) to identify the needs, possibilities and resources of Maynard regarding community preservation. Town funding from a property tax surcharge supports the CPC's efforts toward acquiring and preserving land for open space and/or recreation, as well as acquiring, preserving and restoring historic resources, structures, artifacts and documents. CPC supported the restoration of the cupola that graces the roof of the Artspace building in 2016.

In 2017, the Maynard Historical Commission proposed and voters approved a "Demolition Delay" by-law. The purpose of the by-law is to stipulate up to a twelve-month delay in demolition of historic buildings, allowing for time to consider less destructive options. The year 2018 saw a continuation of the Maynard Historical Properties Survey, with historical information and photograph incorporated in the state's Massachusetts Cultural Resource Information System (MACRIS).

Collectively, all this means that although Maynard is not historically famous as Lexington and Concord, a combination of government and nongovernment efforts have been made to identify and preserve what history Maynard has.

A TWENTY-FIRST-CENTURY POPULATION BOOM

Maynard's history as a nineteenth-century mill town versus the farm towns that gradually morphed into bedroom suburbs had repercussions in the twenty-first century. According to 2016 data, housing in Maynard represented a low-cost hole in the middle of the high-cost donut of Concord, Acton, Stow and Sudbury. Median home values were $361,900 (Maynard), $868,300, $620,900, $579,700 and $826,800, respectively. A preponderance of small houses on small lots made Maynard attractive as a first-home community, as evidenced by weekend flows of stroller pushers. Starting in 2004, a new wave of apartment building and condominium construction added housing options for people who did not want a house and a yard.

The result was population growth after a very long period of stasis. From 1970 through 2010, the population of Maynard hovered above or below 10,000. There was actually a 3 percent decline from 2000 to 2010. School enrollment bottomed in the 2010–11 year. Subsequently, school enrollment rose, and an interim census put the 2015 population at 10,676. The Massachusetts Department of Transportation had estimated a 2020 count of 10,750; the town estimated that it would surpass 11,000 by 2022. Those estimates ended up being conservative, as housing projects that were

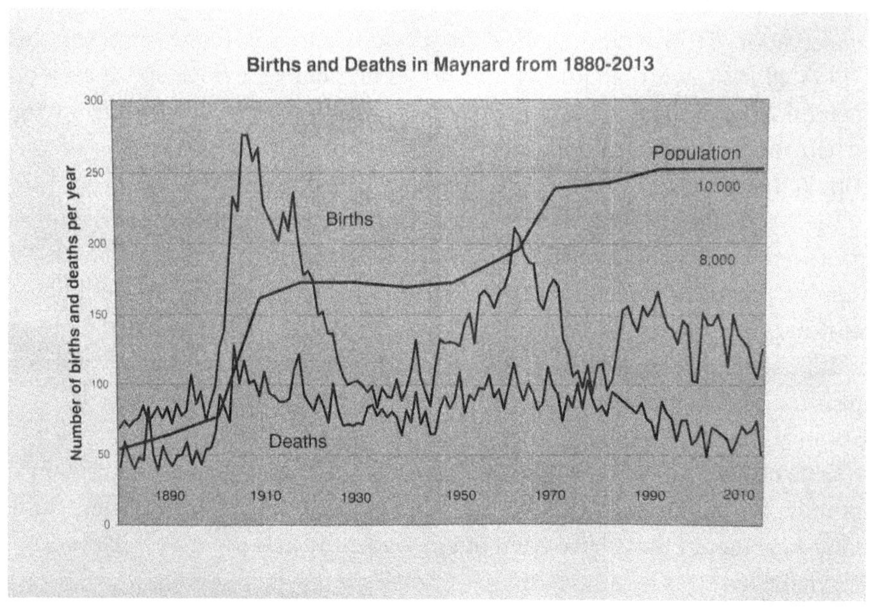

Town of Maynard annual reports list numbers of births and deaths each year. This figure shows steep population increases after the American Woolen Company bought the mill in 1899 and again in the 1960s when Digital Equipment Corporation was growing. Births followed immigrant influx (1900–1930) and the "baby boom" after World War II. There was a spike in deaths marking the Spanish flu pandemic of 1918–19.

not part of those calculations came to fruition. At 129 Parker Street, the apartment complex and independent living center for older residents added a combined 323 living units. Small condominium complexes were wedged into long-empty lots or as conversions—the American Legion building being one example. Lastly, the potential remains for the owners of the mill complex to create housing opportunities, either as building conversion or new construction.

ARTSPACE AND ACME THEATER

In the 1990s, the Town of Maynard decided to explore the idea of supporting the presence of artists in its midst. The catalyst was deciding what to do with a surplus school. Construction of Fowler Middle School on the south side of town meant that the old complex on Summer Street, with parts dating back to 1916, would stand empty. Maynard already had the bad example of an empty ex-school with the Roosevelt School building, which was progressively decaying since closing in 1988 (finally resurrected, phoenix-like, as Maynard Public Library in 2006).

Ideas for what to do with the old Fowler school had come from two directions. First, the town voted to appoint a Fowler School Building Reuse Committee in 1996. Second, a handful of local artists, the self-named Assabet River Artists Association, had begun an effort to create a group identity. Among them were Darthea Cross, Bruce Lucier and Sara Matias. ARAA members and other artists in town, such as photographer Erik Hansen, were sounded out about interest in studio space. The committee reached a conclusion in 1999 that the only realistic plan was to lease the space to a nonprofit arts/cultural group.

The official assignment of this town-owned building to ArtSpace Inc. took place in January 2001. Today, ArtSpace—rebranded in 2019 as "artspace"—provides forty-three studio spaces for about eighty artists. Demand remains high, with perhaps one or two studios becoming available each year. Priority is given to Maynard residents. Rent for the artists is below commercial rates. Rent covers operating costs and staff salaries. The executive directors have been Jero Nesson (2001–14), Linda Spear (2015–19) and, as of the fall of 2019, Jerry Beck. In addition to the studios, the artspace gallery is a wonderful exhibition and lecture space presenting new and important contemporary art by both in-house and nationally known artists. All this offers a wonderful—and free—opportunity to see art, chat with artists and buy their art.

Acme Theater Productions

Currently inhabiting basement space at artspace, Acme has a longer history than its host. Acme began in 1992. Prior to 2000, it was a troupe without a home, rehearsing where it could, storing props and scenery wherever it could and performing at schools and other public spaces. The troupe took on the slogan "Home of the Misfits" to reflect its can-do (with less) attitude. Despite lack of a permanent space, ATP produced award-winning plays and traveled nationally and even internationally.

David Sheppard, founder and executive director of Acme Theater Productions, has been with Acme since day one. Per the Acme website, he provides the group with vision, creative energy and a commitment to quality and has won numerous director awards. In 2001, Acme formally became a nonprofit corporation and, as such, became eligible for space at artspace. All hands, including a few hammered thumbs, converted the ex-school's ex-woodshop into a seventy-seat theater. Sheppard characterized their space as "dark, downstairs—and much loved." Typically, Acme puts on four productions per year. Acme can be thought of as the successor to the Maynard Dramatic Club, an amateur group that had theater productions from 1936 to 1972 and officially disbanded in November 1983. Earlier theater groups dated as far back as 1895.

CULTURAL COUNCIL/CULTURAL DISTRICT

The Maynard Cultural Council channels thousands of dollars of state money every year via grants to support arts, humanities and science programs benefiting the Maynard community. The council—our local arm of the Massachusetts Cultural Council—was also instrumental in applying our cultural district designation, which encompasses and supports cultural, historical and recreational facilities, including the Maynard Public Library, Acme Theatre, artspace, art galleries, the Fine Arts Theatre and other performance spaces, several live music venues and access to the Assabet River Rail Trail.

The state program had its beginnings in 1975 as Artist Fellowships, funded by the Massachusetts Council on the Arts and Humanities. The organization morphed into the Massachusetts Cultural Council in 1990. Going forward, the state continued to award fellowships but also expanded a Local Cultural Council program, which award millions of dollars every year to towns and cities that have their own cultural councils.

The Maynard Cultural Council, a volunteer organization appointed by the board of selectmen, accepts proposals once per year. One of the better-known recent projects was "Maynard as a Canvas," which hired mural artists to create murals on both sides of the one-time Murphy & Snyder Printers building at the corner of Parker and Waltham Streets. Two entries were selected as winners from eighty-some applicants. Completed in 2018, one side features hummingbirds, while the other incorporates portraits of Henry David Thoreau and Babe Ruth. Why those two figures? Because both had visited here—in 1851 and 1917, respectively.

March 2017 saw the culmination of a multi-year effort to apply for and achieve state cultural designation. The application process started years

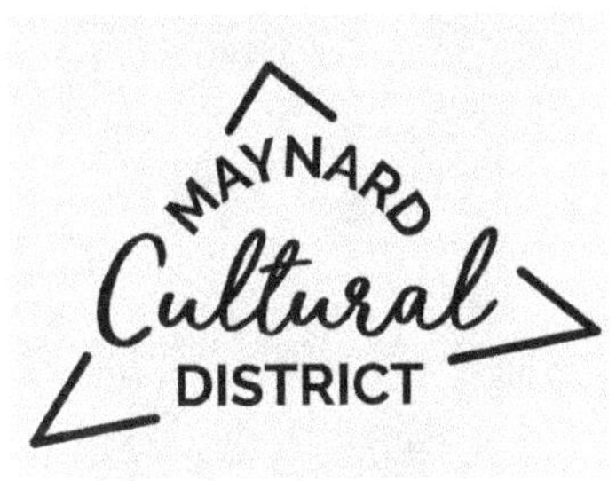

The logo for Maynard's cultural district is symbolic of the district's core triangle formed by Main, Summer and Nason Streets.

earlier, with the formal submittal of the application to the state cultural council in early 2016. This designation was seen as a tremendous boost to Maynard's growing reputation as a cultural destination, a place where residents and visitors alike can stroll from venue to venue, whether their intent is dinner, a film festival, a pub crawl, Maynard Fest or other events. Public events foster a sense of community. As an annual event, the council and district join the Town of Maynard in sponsoring ArtWeek, held from the end of April into early May.

The district designation was initially Assabet Village Cultural District, but in early 2019, it was changed to the more easily identified Maynard Cultural District. The footprint of the district encompasses Summer Street from Waltham Street Bridge to artspace on the north side (with a bulge to capture the library); then south on Florida Road and west on Railroad Street to gather in Main Street, the millpond and the mill complex; and then east along the river to return to Waltham Street. Doing so captures the smaller triangle of Summer, Nason and Main Streets within a larger triangle of the town's central business district. Going forward, the council, district and town will work jointly to enrich Maynard's arts and entertainment experience.

ALWAYS CHANGING

Various volunteer groups have on their own initiative acted in ways that contribute to making Maynard interesting.

Maynard Rocks

This effort started as a small thing and turned into an avalanche. Peter Morgan, resident of Maynard and parent of two school-age daughters, had traveled to Tacoma, Washington, in 2017 on a business trip. There, out for a walk, he spied several small painted rocks lodged in the gaps of a stone wall.

Star Wars is a popular theme for painters of Maynard Rocks.

He brought one home. In April 2017, he and his wife, Andrea, and their daughters started Maynard Rocks, mirroring it after Tacoma Rocks. The genesis of these "Rocks" programs goes back to the Kindness Rocks Project, started by Megan Murphy on Cape Cod ("created to spread inspiration and a moment of kindness for unsuspecting recipients through random inspirational rocks dropped along the way").

Locally, participants are encouraged to paint and place rocks in public places where they will be seen by vigilant passersby. People are advised at the "Maynard Rocks" Facebook page to leave found stones in place, move those to a new spot or replace with one of their own, keeping the found one instead. Photos can be added to the Facebook page. Contributors have ranged from young children taking a paintbrush in hand for the first time to experienced artists. The Morgans hosted rock painting events, and some of Maynard's businesses held Maynard Rocks parties. Recognition of the impact Maynard Rocks has had on making Maynard interesting was recognized by the Maynard Cultural Council.

artspace Outdoors

This space has been a great addition to Maynard's public art since 2016. The idea originated at the behest of then artspace executive director Linda Spear. Artist/tenants formed a Grounds Art Committee. Each year, the committee conducts a juried selection of sculpture proposals submitted by Massachusetts artists. Entries are due in March, work is installed in April and the show lasts through October. Work must be suitable for outdoor conditions, safe for viewers to touch and not susceptible to damage from that touching. During the summer of 2019, about thirty works were on display. Going forward, plans are to expand outdoor art to town public spaces.

Also gracing the artspace front lawn is Maynard's only public labyrinth. Volunteers cut the pattern out of the sod, laid down a layer of stone dust and then installed more than five hundred rough-hewn granite blocks to create a seven-ringed labyrinth thirty feet across. From the artist: "There is no right or wrong way to walk the labyrinth path.…You may want to reflect on where you are in your life…or simply let your thoughts go and quiet your mind. When you reach the center, take some time to reflect, if you wish. The labyrinth is a metaphor for the journey of life."

After many years of entertaining both children and adults, the stones gradually sank into the lawn. Restoration is planned for 2021.

Lisa Bailey took a moment from her Maynard Cultural Council–funded project to run upstairs into the artspace building and take a picture of some of her volunteer labor force at work in the summer of 2007. *Photo by Lisa Bailey.*

Trail of Flowers

Once the Assabet River Rail Trail (ARRT) was paved, a proposal was made to embellish the trail with extensive plantings of spring-blooming bulbs, flowering annuals and flowering perennial flowers, bushes and trees. The Town of Maynard approved. Key questions were asked and answered: Will this cost the town any money? No. Will this require the Department of Public Works to do any planting or maintenance? No. Will this interfere with DPW's intent to mow the borders of the trail? No. This is a great idea!

In the fall of 2018, donations from Maynard Community Gardeners and the Assabet River Rail Trail organization paid for the purchase of two thousand daffodil bulbs, and there were requests for volunteers to plant them. Daffodils were chosen because deer will eat tulips. A planting weekend in October was designated as BYOS ("bring your own shovel"). The spring bloom, the first week of May, was celebrated with a flower-viewing trail walk. For the second and third annual fall plantings, the Maynard Cultural Council awarded $500 grants. Volunteers

May 2019 saw the blooming of hundreds of daffodil bulbs planted at the Marble Farm historic site (just before north end of Maynard's part of the Rail Trail).

planted thousands of bulbs in Maynard and Acton, with Hudson and Marlborough to be added in the future. Spring plantings of pollinator-friendly plants were added starting 2020.

Bicycling Around Town

Maynard offers the Assabet River Rail Trail and a "Complete Streets" program that provides safe and accessible options for walking and biking in addition to motorized vehicles. The Maynard/Stow end of the Rail Trail connects to trails in the Assabet River National Wildlife Refuge. There are also miles of trails in town-owned woods. The Complete Streets principles contribute toward the safety, health, economic viability and quality of life in a community by providing alternative means of travel between home, school, work, recreation and retail destinations.

Maynard Fest and Farmers' Market

The sesquicentennial year of 2021 will mark the twenty-ninth Maynard Fest, an all-day event presented in early October by the Assabet Valley Chamber of Commerce. Live music, nonprofit organization booths, local businesses and out-of-town vendors of crafts are all on display. The event punctuates the end of the Maynard Farmers' Market season, an organization that has been providing people with the opportunity to buy Massachusetts-grown foods and crafts from local artists since 1996. The market starts its season at the end of June, appearing every Saturday in the parking lot by the millpond. Live music and children's activities complement the vendors' offerings.

Master Plan 2020

Maynard's last Master Plan, issued in 1991, was designed to cover fifteen years. After a long and unintentional hiatus, Maynard restarted a Master Plan process in the winter of 2017, resulting in a 2020 Master Plan that will serve as a roadmap for the next twenty years. This plan is Maynard's vision for the future and strategic outline for implementation. Per state law requirements, it addressed natural resources, economic development, infrastructure, transportation, historic and cultural resources, open space

At town meetings, these baskets are used to collect residents' paper votes. The process of conducting town meetings was codified in 1715 by the British Crown Colony of Massachusetts. Articles for discussion and vote must be previously published in a warrant. Maynard's first town meeting was held on April 27, 1871, eight days after it officially became a town.

and recreation, land use and housing; lastly, it provides for a periodically updated action plan to implement goals. The plan calls for promoting a high-density, mixed-use core while preserving greenspace as urban tree planting, parks and forests. The Complete Streets policy that was begun in 2016 will continue to promote a street and sidewalk network for vehicles, cyclists and pedestrians. The addition of the Assabet River Rail Trail in 2018 generated interest in expanding the network. The town encourages housing growth that fits into Maynard's core walkability and also contributes to Maynard reaching the state goal of 10 percent affordable housing. This goal is implemented in large part via the town's "Housing Production Plan," adopted in 2016 and renewed every five years. The plan also recognized the designation by the state of the Maynard Cultural District in 2017, an acknowledgement of the importance of Maynard's performing and visual arts, dining and entertainment businesses in making the town an attractive place to work, live and visit.

Challenges faced by Maynard include an aging infrastructure, potential limits on water supply, the need for more services for the fast-growing senior population, a school system with capacity issues and an antiquated fire station that no longer meets needs. The 129 Parker Street complex added to the tax base while providing mitigation for the impact on traffic and town services.

BIBLIOGRAPHY

Books and Documents

Allison, David. "Transcript of an Oral History Interview with Ken Olsen Digital Equipment Corporation." *American Wool and Cotton Reporter*, September 25, 1902, page 8; October 2, 1902, page 25.

Boothroyd, Paul, and Lewis Halprin. *Assabet Mills*. Images of America. Charleston, SC: Arcadia Publishing, 1999.

———. *Maynard*. Postcard History Series. Charleston, SC: Arcadia Publishing, 2005.

———. *Maynard Massachusetts*. Images of America. Charleston, SC: Arcadia Publishing, 1999.

Coen, Elisabeth. *Ken Olsen: Visionary Scientist, Entrepreneur and Founder of Digital Equipment Corporation*. Wenham, MA: Gordon College Press, 2010.

Earls, Alan R. *Digital Equipment Corporation*. Images of America. Charleston, SC: Arcadia Publishing, 2004.

Gutteridge, William H. *A Brief History of the Town of Maynard, Massachusetts.* Maynard, MA: Town of Maynard, 1921.

Hudson, Alfred. *The Annals of Sudbury, Wayland, and Maynard, Middlesex County, Massachusetts*. N.p., 1891.

Information Technology & Society, National Museum of American History, Smithsonian Institution. 1988.

Liedes, Lisa A., ed. *The Finnish Imprint: A New England Experience*. New York Mills, MN: Parta Printers Inc., 1982.

Mark, David. *Hidden History of Maynard*. Charleston, SC: The History Press, 2014.

———. *Maynard: History and Life Outdoors*. Charleston, SC: The History Press, 2011.

Pearson, Jamie Parker, ed. *Digital at Work: Snapshots from the First Thirty-Five Years.* Burlington, MA: Digital Press, 1992.

Schein, Edgar H. *DEC Is Dead, Long Live DEC: The Lasting Legacy of Digital Equipment Corporation*. Oakland, CA: Berrett-Koehler Publishers, 2004.

Sheridan, Ralph. *A History of Maynard, 1871–1971*. Maynard, MA: Town of Maynard Historical Committee, 1971.

Voogd, Jan. *Maynard, Massachusetts: A House in the Village.* Charleston, SC: The History Press, 2007.

Walker, Barbara A., and W.C. Hanson. "Valuing Differences at Digital Equipment Corporation." In *Diversity in the Workplace*. Edited by S.E. Jackson. New York: Guilford Press. 1992.

Zwinger, Ann, and Edwin Way Teale. *A Conscious Stillness: Two Naturalists on Thoreau's Rivers*. New York: Harper & Row, 1982.

Websites

City-Data. http://www.city-data.com/city/Maynard-Massachusetts.html.

Massachusetts Historical Society. http://www.masshist.org.

Maynard Historical Society. http://maynardhistory.org.

The Maynard Web. https://web.maynard.ma.us/history.

The Maynard Web/The Town Clock. https://web.maynard.ma.us/history/clock1.htm.

Organization for the Assabet, Sudbury and Concord Rivers. http://wwwoars3rivers.org.

Stow Historical Society. http://stowhistoricalsociety.org.

Sudbury Historical Society. http://www.sudbury01776.org.

ABOUT THE SESQUICENTENNIAL STEERING COMMITTEE

In September 2017 the Town of Maynard established a Sesquicentennial Steering Committee to plan for and manage the pending celebrations of the 150th anniversary of the creation of Maynard, April 19, 1871. After some resignations and additions, the Committee members included Molly Bergin, Lisa Dahill, Charles Caragianes, Paula Copley, Ellen Duggan, Dave Griffin, Donald James, David A. Mark, Lindsay McConchie and Jen Picorelli. Meetings are organized under Massachusetts' Open Meeting Law. Postings of meeting dates, agendas and minutes can be found on the Committee's page on the Town of Maynard website. In 2020 the Committee oversaw production of T-shirts and sweatshirts, mugs and flags to sell as souvenirs—also this book—as means of raising money to pay for the celebration events planned for 2021, including a parade and concert.

www.ingramcontent.com/pod-product-compliance
Lightning Source LLC
Chambersburg PA
CBHW070927150426
42812CB00049B/1536

9781540245434